Best-Loved Art from American Museums

Best-Loved Art from American Museums

PATRICIA FAILING

An Artnews Book

 Clarkson N. Potter, Inc./Publishers NEW YORK
DISTRIBUTED BY CROWN PUBLISHERS, INC.

Henri Matisse
Girl with Green Eyes

SAN FRANCISCO MUSEUM OF MODERN ART

The year he painted *Girl with Green Eyes,* Henri Matisse (1869–1954) wrote, "Expression, for me, does not reside in passions glowing in a human face or manifested by a violent movement. The entire arrangement of my picture is expressive: the place occupied by the figures, the empty spaces around them, everything has its share."

Girl with Green Eyes demonstrates his point of view: Although devoid of psychological characterization, *Girl* is an evocative and energetic portrayal. Matisse accomplishes this effect through contrasts of bright colors and interplay of strong organic patterns in both foreground and background sections of the picture. A cast of a Parthenon torso and three strongly ornamented vases on a shelf behind the sitter's head enliven the static forms of face and hat, while the figured embroidery of the Chinese robe serves to activate the lower foreground of the canvas.

Alfred Barr, founding director of New York's Museum of Modern Art, observed that in Matisse's portraits of the years 1908 to 1910 one cannot "assume that the physiognomy of the sitter has been recorded with any degree of accuracy. . . . Yet, to quote the title of a homily Matisse was to deliver ten years later, 'Exactitude is not Truth,' and these ten or so images of women among Matisse's family and friends and models remain among the most vivid and memorable portraits of the period."

1908; Oil on canvas; 26 × 20 inches
Bequest of Harriet Lane Levy

Artnews Books is the imprint of
Annellen Publications, Inc.
5 West 37th Street
New York, New York 10018

Published by Clarkson N. Potter, Inc.,
One Park Avenue,
New York, New York 10016
and simultaneously in Canada by General Publishing Company Limited

Manufactured in Hong Kong

Library of Congress Cataloging in Publication Data
Failing, Patricia.
   Best-loved art from American Museums
   1. Art—United States—Public opinion.
2. Art museums—United States—Visitors.   I. Title.
N6505.F34   1983   708.13   83-13987
ISBN 0-517-55168-3

10 9 8 7 6 5 4 3 2 1
First Edition

CONTENTS

INTRODUCTION

OF THE THOUSANDS OF WORKS OF ART in a museum there are inevitably a few—sometimes one above all—toward which many visitors develop definite feelings of attachment. What are these works of art? What accounts for their broad attraction? More than sixty museums in the United States and Canada were asked these questions regarding their own permanent collections. The fifty-seven museums that responded all replied to the first question and most addressed the second as well.

How were museums able to make these decisions? Most used some combination of the following criteria: postcard and reproduction sales, visitor comment cards, staff interviews, docent surveys, audience polls, and even the number of complaints received when certain works were temporarily removed from exhibition. As several respondents pointed out, postcard and reproduction sales provide a strong indication of what visitors want especially to remember, but some objects do not reproduce well and no museum offers reproductions of every item in its collection. Postcard and reproduction sales, therefore, provide limited information that must be checked against other sources. The accuracy of any or all of these indicators is by no means unquestionable, but nearly all the country's major museums felt sufficiently knowledgeable about viewer opinion to confine their replies to a narrow range of work, often a single example.

Certain institutions replied with several selections, among them the Art Institute of Chicago, the Metropolitan Museum of Art, the Whitney Museum of American Art, the Los Angeles County Museum of Art, and the Solomon R. Guggenheim Museum. Others, including such large and encyclopedic museums as the National Gallery of Art, the Museum of Fine Arts in Boston, the Cleveland Museum of Art, and the Philadelphia Museum of Art, reported that visitors felt most strongly about a single work.

The fifty-seven museums that participated in the survey are represented by seventy-seven works of art. The most frequently chosen artist in the group is Auguste Renoir (five paintings), followed by American painter John Singer Sargent and another Frenchman, Claude Monet (three paintings each). Fifty-nine selections are paintings, eight are sculptures, eight are classified as textiles and decorative arts, and two are full-scale environments. A single work, *The Voyage of Life* by the American artist Thomas Cole, consists of four separate but related paintings.

Of the paintings, thirty can be generally described as depicting figures in various settings, twenty-two of them outdoor and eight indoor. The remainder includes eleven portraits, twelve landscapes, four abstract or semiabstract compositions, and two still lifes. Most of the paintings are large; the greatest expanse of canvas is Emanuel Leutze's *Washington Crossing the Delaware,* measuring twelve feet five inches high by twenty-one feet three inches long.

The works range chronologically from the fourth century B.C.—*The Getty Bronze,* attributed to Lysippos—to the Hudson River Museum's 1979 bookstore environment by Red Grooms. A majority of the works were created in the nineteenth century, followed closely by the twentieth. The most typical work in the survey, therefore, would be a large nineteenth-century painting of figures in a landscape.

What is known about the viewers whose opinions the museums are reporting? There are a great many of them, and most are repeat visitors. Some institutions cited an in-depth study conducted by the National Research Center of the Arts in 1975, which revealed that 65 million Americans—43 percent of the population—had visited an art museum or gallery in the year preceding the survey. (Though no comparable study has been made recently, reports received by the American Council of Museums indicate a steady increase in art museum attendance nationwide.) Those who had gone to an art museum went four times a year on average. This confirms the experience reported by several museums: repeat visitors will often notice when objects in the permanent collection are moved or loaned, and therefore inquire about their status.

The viewer whose opinion the museums reported is likely to be well educated. The National Research Center study showed that among college graduates, 78 percent had visited an art museum at least once during the preceding year. Many patronize museum bookstores and attend museum education programs, which have drawn increasing numbers of participants in recent years. They seek further information about objects toward which they are particularly drawn; in some cases museums have responded by publishing special booklets or guides. These viewers will also go to museums to see specific works of art; several institutions characterize their selections as "pilgrimage pictures" which visitors are known to make a point of seeing.

Viewer interest is also affected by broad social trends. Government funding in the last fifteen years has dramatically increased the number of art programs in smaller communities and has provided many established museums with incentives for audience development. The investment value of fine art in an inflationary economy has attracted corporations as well as greater numbers of individuals to the field of art collecting and has enhanced the social status of collecting. The less affluent can avail themselves of a wider range of reasonably priced art books and reproductions. There are more professional artists in the United States than ever before and a greater variety of art classes offered for all age groups.

The opinions of today's viewers can be compared in certain respects with those expressed in a similar survey conducted in the early 1950s by *Time* magazine. *Time* polled forty-five museums and college galleries, publishing the results at irregular intervals from August 1951 to November 1955. The project was coordinated by *Time* art critic Alexander Eliot, an amateur painter and great-grandson of Harvard University president and prolific writer Charles Eliot. When the series was initiated with Renoir's *A Girl with a Watering Can* from the National Gallery of Art, Eliot listed the following bases for its selection: the painting, he wrote, "leads gallery reproduction sales, guides are questioned about it constantly and copyists prefer it above all others."

The *Time* sample included a number of small municipal galleries, some of which subsequently evolved into different institutions, and did not include many of the country's major museums. Comparisons with the 1950s survey must therefore be qualified by noting that a different group of museums was contacted in each survey. Another complication is the growth of permanent collections and the establishment of new museums since the 1950s. Keeping these considerations in mind, one striking difference between the *Time* survey and the present selection is the number of paintings with overtly religious subject matter in the *Time* group—six of the forty-six paintings. None appear in the present survey.

Another difference is the smaller number of choices with an evident relationship to local history in the *Time* group. In the present survey, several museums linked viewer reaction to historical circumstance: Edgar Degas' *Portrait of Estelle Musson* from the New Orleans Museum of Art, for example, was purchased by public subscription as a remembrance of the artist's visit to New Orleans in 1872. Nostalgia for the gold rush era draws California viewers to Charles Christian Nahl's *Sunday Morning in the Mines* at the Crocker Art Museum in Sacramento. A similar nostalgia attends George Caleb Bingham's Missouri River scene, *The Jolly Flatboatmen in Port*, at the Saint Louis Art Museum and the wooden figure of *Captain Jinks* in the Newark Museum, which stood for years outside a Newark cigar store. Tom Thompson's and Emily Carr's paintings commemorate the great wildernesses integral to Canadian national identity, while the Blackfoot quilled shirt at the Glenbow Foundation in Calgary reminds viewers of the achievements of the region's indigenous culture. The choice of the *Hand Scroll of Deer and Poems* by Seattle Art Museum audiences attests to the Japanese influence on the Pacific Northwest. Finally, in some areas viewers have an especially strong admiration for local artists who have earned national reputations, such as Robert Indiana at the Indianapolis Museum of Art and Paul Manship at the Minnesota Museum of Art.

Perhaps more interesting than the differences between the two surveys are the similarities. Renoir was the most frequently named artist in both cases. Of the ten paintings that appear in both surveys, four are by Renoir: *A Girl with a Watering Can*, the National Gallery of Art; *Romaine Lacaux*, the Cleveland Museum of Art; *The Dance at Bougival*, Boston, Museum of Fine Arts; *Luncheon of the Boating Party*, the Phillips Collection. Other repeats are El Greco's *View of Toledo*, the Metropolitan Museum of Art; Pieter Bruegel's *The Wedding Dance*, the Detroit Institute of Arts; Thomas Gainsborough's, *Blue Boy*, the Huntington Library; Frederick Edwin Church's *Niagara*, Corcoran Museum of Art; George Bellows's, *Dempsey and Firpo*, Whitney Museum of American Art; and John Singer Sargent's *El Jaleo* from the Isabella Stewart Gardner Museum.

Exceptional admiration for a number of these paintings is long-standing. Church's *Niagara* was exhibited to huge crowds in London and Paris in 1857, Sargent's *El Jaleo* was the picture of the year at the Paris Salon of 1882, large editions of *Dempsey and Firpo* lithographs were sold in the 1920s, and the public followed with great interest Henry Huntington's purchase of the already famed *Blue Boy* in 1921.

A number of museums in the current survey offered suggestions about why their visitors might be especially drawn to certain objects. Setting can play a part: many of the selections are prominently placed or isolated within their galleries. It is also clear that viewer identification with local artists, subject matter, or regional history is often an important factor. Another point repeatedly mentioned was admiration for technical skill, although no respondent said that technique alone was sufficient to explain the rapport viewers develop with certain works. Several museums suggested that vicarious enjoyment of the artist's emotion—tenderness, affection, *joie de vivre*—might be a contributing factor, while others saw an inherently mysterious subject matter as a possible basis for personal involvement. Fantasy and amusement play a role, as does nostalgia. But only one observation, made in reference to Monet's *Water Lilies* at the Portland Art Museum, seems to apply in nearly all cases: they "reward prolonged viewing to an unusual degree."

Assessing the seventy-seven choices as a whole, it does not seem unreasonable to conclude that, in most instances, viewers are essentially reacting to the timeless and universal qualities possessed by great works of art. The survey results indicate a considerable degree of concord between artistic excellence and broad-based appreciation; with few exceptions, the choices in this survey are also ranked as major achievements by scholars of art history. All the artworks are strong visual statements that can be enjoyed without knowledge of their art historical context, although they frequently inspire viewers to seek further information about them. The basis of appreciation often differs from that of the experienced connoisseur, but the judgment of today's average museum visitor may be much more sophisticated than is generally supposed.

—*Patricia Failing*

Best-Loved Art from American Museums

Europe:
The Classical Tradition

Artist Unknown
Archangel Raphael

LOS ANGELES COUNTY MUSEUM OF ART

The *Archangel Raphael* was created by an unknown master who probably worked in Naples late in the sixteenth century. Neapolitan churches of the period were noted for their elaborate wooden icons, a taste cultivated by the Spanish Hapsburgs who then ruled the city. Images of Raphael held special significance for Neapolitan society: Old Testament Apocrypha identify Raphael as the ideal guardian of human spirits and in Naples he was regarded as the special protector of seafaring travelers and sailors.

An indentation in the base of the sculpture indicates that the archangel was originally accompanied by another figure, most likely the young Tobias, hero of the apocryphal Book of Tobit. Legend has it that Tobias, sent by his blind father to conduct business in a distant city, was accompanied on his journey by the angel Raphael, disguised as a fellow traveler. Under the guidance of Raphael, Tobias safely completed his mission, triumphed over a demon, acquired a wife, and returned to cure his father's blindness. In Renaissance Italy the theme of Tobias and the angel was often chosen by a family to commemorate the travels of a son, who might be represented as Tobias.

The Los Angeles *Raphael* is life-sized and further distinguished by its remarkable state of preservation. Polychromed icons were typically repainted from time to time to freshen the colors, a practice that eventually results in an accumulation of paint layers that obscures the details of the carving. The Los Angeles work has been gilded and painted only once, the colors having retained most of their original intensity. The wooden surface was first covered with a layer of gesso or stucco; the wings, hair, and drapery were then completely gilded. The gilt of the robe and tunic was painted over, and designs and patterns were created by lightly scratching away the paint to reveal the gold below. The underlying gilt produces a chromatic effect reminiscent of precious stones, which enhances by contrast the warmth of the painted flesh. The wings, hinged to move forward and backward, repeat the gentle curves of the patterned drapery and frame the graceful twists of head, torso, and stance. The result is a subtle interplay of stillness and animation that expresses the angel's dual attributes of capability and benevolence and establishes the *Archangel Raphael* as a masterly example of visionary art.

Late sixteenth century; Polychromed wood; height 70 inches
Gift of Anna Bing Arnold

El Greco
View of Toledo

THE METROPOLITAN MUSEUM OF ART · NEW YORK CITY

French and American artists of the late nineteenth century played a major role in reviving the reputation of Doménikos Theotokópoulis (1541–1614), known as El Greco. One of them was the American Impressionist Mary Cassatt, who recommended that her collector friends Henry and Louisine Havemeyer seek out El Greco's canvases when the couple toured Spain shortly after the turn of the century. The Havemeyers developed an immediate enthusiasm for El Greco and purchased three of his most important pictures, including *View of Toledo,* which was bequeathed to the Metropolitan Museum in 1929.

It has long been acknowledged that the electrifying *View of Toledo* is factually inaccurate. Students of Spanish art typically attribute the distortions to the artist's irrational mysticism, a conjecture linked to the presence in Toledo of Saint Teresa of Avila and Saint John of the Cross while El Greco lived there. New York University art historian Jonathan Brown recently proposed another interpretation. Brown locates *View of Toledo* within the now-forgotten sixteenth-century genre of the emblematic city view. In contrast to cartographic cityscapes intended to serve as accurate records of urban topography, the emblematic view selectively emphasizes the city's most important natural and architectural features as symbols of its wealth, power, or beauty. El Greco's emblematic composition suggests Toledo's status as an earthly City of God. The most prominently featured buildings are the cathedral and the royal palace, whose positions El Greco reversed. He eliminated the medieval city wall and rerouted the Tagus River to the west, intensifying the dramatic setting of the hilltop structures. Above all the sulfurous rolling clouds attest to the presence of heavenly forces, an interpretation supported by El Greco's inclusion of an identical city view in the background of *Saint Joseph and the Christ Child,* an altarpiece he later painted for the Chapel of San José in Toledo.

Ca. 1595; Oil on canvas; 47¾ × 42¾ inches
Bequest of Mrs. H. O. Havemeyer, 1929. The H. O. Havemeyer Collection

Pieter Bruegel The Elder
The Wedding Dance

THE DETROIT INSTITUTE OF ARTS

One of the most popular painters of any period or nationality, the Flemish artist Pieter Bruegel (1525/1530–1569) has been widely misunderstood. For many years he was believed to be a peasant, but recent scholarship acknowledges his high level of education, his personal association with leading humanists of his time, and his patronage by the Hapsburg court in Brussels. Bruegel's scenes of peasant life are noted for their detailed reportage and droll characterization, yet, as one of his close friends wrote at the time of the artist's death, "In all his works more is implied than is depicted."

In the case of *The Wedding Dance,* less attention has been paid to its allegorical dimensions than to its formal structure. Bruegel was obsessed with the problem of representing movement and experimented constantly with new solutions. In *The Wedding Dance* the dancers weave back and forth across the painting in rhythmical bounces, their animation heightened by the two groups of static figures in the upper third of the canvas. As a unit the dancers form a kind of flying wedge moving deep into pictorial space, augmenting the overall dynamism of the composition.

In its loosely dispersed crowd structure, bird's-eye perspective, and meticulous detail, *The Wedding Dance* has antecedents in the work of Hieronymus Bosch (ca. 1450–1516), but the minimally modeled figures and witty depiction of rural types and costumes have little precedent in Flemish art. Bruegel's preoccupation with peasant life seems to have arisen from a complex view of Christian humanism which distanced him from his subjects and yet drew him to the universality of their follies. Perhaps it is this delicately balanced satire—uncompromising but not malicious—that has long nourished Bruegel's popular acclaim.

Ca. 1566; Oil on canvas; 47 × 62 inches
City of Detroit Purchase

Peter Paul Rubens
Prometheus Bound

PHILADELPHIA MUSEUM OF ART

Ranked by the painter himself as one of "the flowers of my stock," *Prometheus Bound* is the product of Peter Paul Rubens's (1577–1640) early career. The life-size figure was painted after his return in 1608 from an eight-year stay in Italy, where he was especially impressed by the scale and color of Venetian painting. Rubens derived the composition of *Prometheus* from a Michelangelo drawing of the myth of Tityus.

The Prometheus and Tityus myths were often merged in the early seventeenth century. Tityus, the son of Earth, assaulted Leto, the mother of Apollo and Artemis. He was killed by Apollo and punished in the underworld by vultures who tore at his liver, thought to be the seat of sexual desire. The crime of Prometheus was the theft of fire, which he gave to man; as punishment Zeus chained Prometheus to the summit of Mount Caucasus where an eagle appeared daily to feed upon his liver, which regenerated overnight.

This amalgamation of the two myths is seen in a seventeenth-century prose poem composed in honor of Rubens's painting by Dutch poet Dominik Baudius, who refers to the eagle as a vulture:

> . . . a ferocious vulture, with his hooked beak searches the chest of Prometheus and gives no respite to his victim: the cruel bird devours again and again his ever-regrowing liver. He is not content with this frightful repast and with his claws tears open his face and body. . . . The spectator imagines he can see him move from side to side and beat the air with his wings . . . and he is seized with horror.

The tension between fascination and horror that Baudius expressed continues to affect those who study the picture both on a scholarly and an informal level. The technical history of the painting provides insights into the means by which the artist achieved this powerful effect. In a letter of 1618, for example, Rubens reveals that the eagle was painted by Frans Snyders, a famous specialist in animal painting. This is the only collaborator Rubens ever mentioned by name. At some point, probably also in 1618, Rubens attached a seventeen-inch-wide strip to the left edge of the canvas, where he clarified Prometheus's identity by adding a fiery torch. The addition also transformed a tightly compressed composition into a more expansive and dramatic design, presaging the baroque style with which Rubens's name has become synonymous.

Ca. 1611; Oil on canvas; 95⅜ × 82½ inches

Rembrandt van Rijn
Portrait of a Young Boy

NORTON SIMON MUSEUM · PASADENA, CALIFORNIA

The subject of *Portrait of a Young Boy* by Rembrandt van Rijn (1606–1669) was once thought to be Prince William of Orange, born in 1650, who later became William III, king of England. This identification is supported by the boy's luxurious costume, the suggestion of an animal or bird perched on the left arm—a traditional seventeenth-century attribute of royal or aristocratic children—and the portrait's formal composition. The free and brushy execution of the painting, in addition, is characteristic of Rembrandt's technique in the mid-1650s when young Prince William would have been the same age as the boy in the picture.

This argument, however, is by no means conclusive. It is unlikely that Rembrandt's connections with the House of Orange were substantial enough in the mid-1650s to support his nomination as portraitist for the prince, and the child's face bears no resemblance to that of young William III in other paintings. Finally, despite its formal composition, the portrait is conceived with an intimacy and charm that not only would have been out of place in a state portrait but also indicates a close and affectionate relationship between the painter and the boy. One can vicariously perceive the warmth that the painter felt for the sitter and it is this intimate quality, the Norton Simon Museum suggests, that draws viewers to the portrait.

Although portrait identifications are not often made on the basis of mood, the evident tenderness of Rembrandt's approach to his subject has led to the supposition that the boy may have been Rembrandt's son, Titus, the only surviving offspring of his marriage to Saskia van Uylenborch. The couple's three other children had all died in early infancy before Titus was born in 1641; Saskia herself died when Titus was but a few months old. An especially affectionate relationship between father and son, therefore, would not have been unlikely. Comparison of the child's features with other portraits identified as Titus indicates a general similarity of appearance. The broad and sketchy execution of the painting, uncharacteristic of the artist's style in the 1640s and thus cited as evidence that the boy is not young Titus, could be accounted for by the fact that the painting is clearly unfinished. As for the costume, the child may well have been fitted out with props from his father's studio—a frequent practice by Rembrandt—in celebration of his first portrait.

Late 1640s (?); Oil on canvas; 25½ × 22 inches
The Norton Simon Foundation, Pasadena

Rembrandt van Rijn
The Polish Rider

THE FRICK COLLECTION · NEW YORK CITY

Most authorities who write about *The Polish Rider* by Rembrandt van Rijn (1606–1669) express the idea that there is something mysterious about the subject of the picture. One of the first and most eloquent of these expressions appears in a review of the first public exhibition of the painting in 1898: "We do not know his name or who he was. In Rembrandt's representation he appears to be a young hero, somewhat like Fridtjof Nansen [the Norwegian explorer who first crossed Greenland's ice cap in 1898], about to proceed on a dangerous mission in a mysterious world of adventure, on his way to conquer unknown realms by virtue of his courage and his genius."

The sense of mystery suggested by the composition has its parallel in the history of the painting. No document survives to tell us when it was painted or for what purpose. The painting was unknown to Rembrandt scholars until the early 1890s when it was discovered in the collection of a Polish count. In 1910 the English critic Roger Fry negotiated the sale of the painting to the American industrialist Henry Clay Frick. When the painting entered Frick's collection conservators discovered that several inches of the original canvas, with two of the horse's hoofs, had been cut from the bottom of the painting and that a strip approximately four inches wide had been added later.

Many attempts have been made to identify the young rider, and most of them based on an analysis of the costume. Dutch and German scholars tend to believe the clothing belonged to a Polish soldier visiting Amsterdam, while Polish experts are of the opinion that the rider was a Dutchman dressed up in a Polish uniform. An American authority on Dutch art, Julius Held, points out that both propositions are based on the erroneous assumption that the figure wears a distinctive uniform corresponding to one worn by a specific military body of the early seventeenth century. There is nothing in the rider's apparel, Held argues, that can be associated with soldiers of a specific nation. Had the painting been found in a Hungarian castle instead of a Polish one, Held maintains, it "might have become famous, with equal if not better right, as *The Hungarian Rider.*"

The skeletal appearance of the horse, the extraordinary handsomeness of the rider, and the suggestions of menace in the landscape have prompted another set of theories which hold that the painting represents a character from history, literature, or mythology. The fact that the rider's identity remains unresolved seems to enhance the picture's fascination. "The picture's meaning continues to defy interpretations," observes Frick curator Edgar Munhall. "People are therefore more prone to give it their own interpretation—always more appealing than scholarly dogma."

Ca. 1665; Oil on canvas; 46 × 53⅛ inches
© The Frick Collection

Jan Vermeer
Young Woman with a Water Jug

THE METROPOLITAN MUSEUM OF ART · NEW YORK CITY

The reputation of Dutch painter Jan Vermeer (1632–1675) as the great master of the interior genre scene is the product of nineteenth- and twentieth-century scholarship. Several theories have been advanced to account for this belated acknowledgment, among them the small number of his paintings (around thirty-five), the uniquely modern quality of his compositional style, the subtlety of his symbolism, and his apparent aloofness from normal social relationships between patron and artist.

With the exception of two cityscapes, all known paintings by Vermeer are indoor scenes or portraits. Each is characterized by an intense feeling for dimension and depth even when figures are positioned in small, confined spaces. In *Young Woman with a Water Jug,* well-defined rectangles of table and map establish the foreground and background limits on the right side of the picture; on the left, dimension is suggested by amorphous shadows, light, and air. On one side sunlight is a complement to matter, highlighting the textures of basin, rug, and chair. On the other, subtle interplays of transparency and reflection focus attention on the qualities of light itself. Such intricately balanced contrasts lead Vermeer scholar Edward Snow to describe the artist as "one of the most profoundly dialectical of painters." Compositions such as *Young Woman with a Water Jug,* Snow continues, "generate conviction in an objective order of things permanently achieved, yet balance it against the impression of a world delicately poised, held as if in the palm of the hand."

Ca. 1665; Oil on canvas; 18 × 16 inches
Gift of Henry G. Marquand, 1889

Nicolas de Largillière
Madame Aubry and Her Son, Léonor

MINNEAPOLIS INSTITUTE OF ARTS

The Aubrys were a wealthy bourgeois family from Tours; Léonor Aubry, father-in-law to the woman in the picture and grandfather of the little boy, served as secretary to Louis XIV, as did the woman's father, Gabriel Coustard, a prosperous Parisian cloth merchant. In the latter half of the seventeenth century, the post of secretary to the king after twenty years' service conferred personal and hereditary nobility and thus was described at the time as *savonnette à vilain*—perfumed soap with which to wash away one's base origins.

Trained in Antwerp, Nicolas de Largillière (1656–1746) became a protégé of the King's First Painter, Charles Le Brun. After seven years' study in London, he returned to Paris, where he quickly gained prominence as a society painter. His portraits were very expensive, and although Largillière is frequently characterized as a portraitist of public officials, wealth seems to have been the sole basis upon which his models were selected. Largillière was engaged to paint four different portraits of the Aubry family in 1699 and 1700, the first commissioned by the elder Léonor Aubry a few months after he, and thus his family, earned the title of nobility.

Three centuries ago, fashions changed almost as quickly as they do today and the aristocratic women whom Largillière painted often attempted to give their portraits a longer life span by having themselves portrayed in the costumes of goddesses or mythological beings. But those with newly acquired nobility and money tended to favor elegant contemporary dress. Catherine Aubry selected a fashionable ultramarine-blue velvet gown lined with flowered brocade and embellished with silver lamé and rose-colored ribbons. As was customary for wealthy five-year-old boys, young Léonor wears a dress and, in this case, a matching vermillion velvet hat. The gray-and-white whippet nuzzling Madame Aubry's left hand may have belonged to the artist, for the same dog appears in other portraits. In these sumptuously rendered costumes, says former curator of painting Gregory Hedberg, mother and son project "a sense of glamour lacking in contemporary society," which places Largillière's portrait among the most widely appreciated artworks at the Minneapolis Institute of Arts.

1700; Oil on canvas; 52⅜ × 14⅞ inches
The John R. Van Derlip Fund

Thomas Gainsborough
The Blue Boy

THE HENRY E. HUNTINGTON LIBRARY AND ART GALLERY · SAN MARINO, CALIFORNIA

Although no other work by a British artist enjoys the fame of *The Blue Boy* by Thomas Gainsborough (1727–1788), the date and subject of the painting have never been conclusively established. The painting apparently attracted little attention during Gainsborough's lifetime, and there are no reliable contemporary references to its origin. The first mention of the sitter's identity appears in Edward Edwards's *Anecdotes of Painters,* published in 1808, twenty years after Gainsborough's death. Edwards states in a footnote, "This was the portrait of a Master Brutall, whose father was a considerable ironmonger, in Greek-street, Soho." Edwards misspelled the name but was clearly referring to Johnathan Buttall, a Soho ironmonger, or hardware merchant, who was Gainsborough's good friend and one of a small group the artist invited to his funeral. The painting was catalogued among Buttall's possessions, furthermore, when financial difficulties forced him to auction his household goods in 1796.

On stylistic grounds the painting is dated after the mid-1760s but before the 1780s. In the 1760s Gainsborough became acquainted with the seventeenth-century portraits of Sir Anthony Van Dyck and developed an unabashed admiration for his predecessor's work. This admiration is clearly visible in *The Blue Boy,* wherein the costume, format, and pose are borrowed directly from Van Dyck. In two other portraits of young boys dated 1773 and 1776, the sitters wear the same Van Dyck costume as does *The Blue Boy,* prompting the supposition that the garment was one of Gainsborough's studio props. These observations, however, compound the problem of *The Blue Boy*'s identity. The boy appears to be—at the oldest—in his teens. Johnathan Buttall was born in 1751 or 1752 and thus would probably have been too old to have worn the costume at the same time as did the other sitters.

Since *The Blue Boy* is unique in Gainsborough's oeuvre, stories have arisen attributing its origin to some sort of artistic challenge rather than to a regular portrait commission. None of these stories can be substantiated, but there is evidence that the painting was not undertaken as a normal commission. X-rays have revealed the beginnings of another portrait of an older man beneath that of the boy. From the position of the older head, it is clear that Gainsborough planned a full-length portrait of an adult and that he cut down the canvas when he used it for *The Blue Boy.* Since artists normally used new canvas for new commissions, Gainsborough's employment of a used, cut-down canvas suggests that the painting was undertaken for the artist's own satisfaction. *The Blue Boy* may thus be a *jeu d'esprit,* Gainsborough's joyful homage to Van Dyck, the artist whom he admired above all others.

Ca. 1770; Oil on canvas; 70 × 48 inches

Francisco de Goya
The Matador Pedro Romero

KIMBELL ART MUSEUM · FORT WORTH, TEXAS

Francisco de Goya's life (1746–1828) was marked by a series of dramatic crises which gave rise to quantum leaps in his artistic development. One of these occurred after a near-fatal illness left him totally deaf when he was forty-five. After his convalescence Goya's work took on a more reflective character, evidenced in his sensitive portrait of the matador Pedro Romero, completed five years later.

Pedro Romero was the grandson of Francisco Romero, patriarch of a major dynasty of matadors who altered the ritual of the bullfight by introducing the *estoque*—the sword used to kill the bull—and the *muleta*—the small red cape used in conjunction with the sword. In the sixteenth and seventeenth centuries bullfighting was a sport of the nobility, performed on horseback with lances. When this practice was abolished by Philip V in the eighteenth century, the bullfight was taken over by young men of the lower classes, among them the Romeros, who fought the animals on foot.

Pedro Romero was Goya's close friend. Goya is said to have been an amateur bullfighter himself, and designed a distinctive professional matador's uniform worn on commemorative occasions.

By his own account, in twenty-eight years of fighting Pedro Romero killed 5,600 bulls without ever being wounded. Praised for the restraint and dignity of his style, Romero was appointed director of the Royal School of Bullfighting in Madrid.

Goya's painting of Romero recedes spatially from the elegant, superbly painted sword hand, a kind of subtle visual irony that was the artist's special province. The daring balance of somber tones and shades of red is a chromatic equivalent of Romero's dramatic profession, a profession demanding an artistic taste for violence not unlike Goya's own.

1795–97; Oil on canvas; 33⅛ × 25⅛ inches

Joseph Mallord William Turner
Dort or Dordrecht, The Dort Packet-Boat from Rotterdam Becalmed

YALE CENTER FOR BRITISH ART
NEW HAVEN, CONNECTICUT

Son of a London barber, Joseph Mallord William Turner (1775–1851) was a proficient draftsman at the age of twelve when tradition has it that his father began selling his drawings to his customers. Turner entered the Royal Academy schools in London when he was fourteen and first exhibited there the following year. After he left the Academy, Turner traveled regularly in search of new landscape subject matter. In 1817 he visited Holland, where he made sketches of the waterfront of Dort, also called Dordrecht, in preparation for this painting.

First shown at the Royal Academy in 1818, *Dort* was acclaimed as "one of the most magnificent pictures ever exhibited" and soon became one of Turner's most famous compositions. A strong demur, however, was entered by the critic John Ruskin, who otherwise argued for Turner's superiority over all other landscape painters. "I never saw any of his work with so little variety of tone in it than this. . . ." said Ruskin. "The sky's the best part of the picture but there is a straggly and artificial look in its upper clouds, quite unusual with Turner."

Modern historians tend to concur with Ruskin on the importance of the sky: *Dort* signals a growing preoccupation with atmospheric light that would dominate the artist's later work and prefigures Impressionism in its dematerialization of physical form. Reputedly one of the artist's personal favorites, *Dort* looks backward to older Dutch marine painters and forward as well, marking the culmination of the first half of Turner's career.

1818; Oil on canvas; 62 × 92 inches
Paul Mellon Collection

33

Adolphe William Bouguereau
The Young Shepherdess

SAN DIEGO MUSEUM OF ART

Around the turn of the century few great American private art collections were without a painting by the French academician Adolphe William Bouguereau (1825–1905). As a young man Bouguereau showed extraordinary talent for drawing the human figure. After study at the École des Beaux-Arts, he won the Prix de Rome in 1850 and was made a chevalier of the Legion of Honor in 1859. Bouguereau's place in history was secured by mythological and genre scenes of the 1870s and 1880s. During these years he developed a warm and sentimental variant of academic classicism especially noted for sensual flesh tones and highly refined execution.

Bouguereau's favorite subjects as a mature artist—cupids, nymphs, and young shepherdesses—recall the rococo taste of the eighteenth century. The shepherdess, a fashionable character since the time of Madame de Pompadour and Marie Antoinette, appears in a number of Bouguereau's pictures. In the San Diego canvas, the idealization of the young girl's face has a counterpart in the timeless peasant costume. Robert Isaacson, an American authority on Bouguereau's work, points out that while such paintings are identified with their era by their overt appeal to the senses, their idealization and avoidance of references to contemporary life tend to set them "in a never-never land of pure beauty."

Bouguereau's tightly finished surfaces began falling out of fashion in the 1880s—Edgar Degas and his younger colleagues condemned any canvas that was highly glossed as *bouguereauté*—"bouguerated." Later it was his choice of sentimental subjects that drew the most criticism, and Bouguereau's name eventually became synonymous with the prostitution of technical skill for commercial gain. This skill, however, ultimately prompted a revived appreciation of his ability to create, in Isaacson's words, "an apotheosis of the ordinary."

1885; Oil on canvas; 62 × 28½ inches
Gift of Mr. and Mrs. Edwin S. Larsen

Lord Frederick Leighton
Flaming June

MUSEO DE ARTE DE PONCE · PONCE, PUERTO RICO

Described by Leighton biographers Leonee and Richard Ormond as the artist's "most uninhibited hymn to human beauty and life itself," *Flaming June* was first exhibited at the London Royal Academy in 1895. The occasion was well remembered by Leighton's (1830–1896) friends, for it marked one of the last public appearances of the dying artist, the academy's president from 1878 until his death.

In his later years, Leighton's name was frequently linked with that of his model for *Flaming June,* Ada Alice Pullan, an actress known as Dorothy Dene. Dene first modeled for Leighton in 1879, and by the mid-1880s had become one of his chief sources of inspiration. Leighton arranged for professional training to augment his cockney model's innate dramatic talent, and in 1885 Dene made her London debut. She was engaged for a number of roles and in 1890 joined the company of the Globe Theatre. But her career floundered despite Leighton's support, and the painter sadly confided to a friend, "My interest in her has been turned to her disadvantage." Leighton, a high-minded, lifelong Victorian bachelor, flatly denied the inevitable rumors of their romantic involvement: Leighton's relationship with his protégée was not unlike that of Henry Higgins and Eliza Doolittle in George Bernard Shaw's *Pygmalion*.

Sleeping or reclining girls are among Leighton's most satisfying subjects. *Flaming June,* despite the figure's acutely bent knees, elbows, and neck, conveys the impression of complete relaxation. Leighton was intrigued by the contrast of animated drapery and inanimate form; his notebooks cite the "fascination in drapery—wayward flow & ripple like living water together with absolute repose." Above all, however, *Flaming June* is memorable for its extremely sensual color—here almost an indulgence for its own sake. This indulgence, together with the mysterious lighting and circular compositions, says Ponce museum director René Taylor, makes *Flaming June* "something of a tour de force."

1895; Oil on canvas; 47½ × 47½ inches
The Luis A. Ferré Foundation

Sir Lawrence Alma-Tadema
Spring

THE J. PAUL GETTY MUSEUM · MALIBU, CALIFORNIA

The highlight of the 1895 Winter Exhibition at London's Royal Academy was *Spring,* the most ambitious product of the immensely successful Sir Lawrence Alma-Tadema (1836–1912). Alma-Tadema specialized in detailed genre paintings of upper-middle-class Greek and Roman citizens, and because his subjects were people involved in common daily activities, critics in the 1890s compared his work favorably with that of the seventeenth-century Dutch painters Pieter de Hooch and Jan Vermeer.

Laurens Alma Tadema was in fact born in the Netherlands and educated in Antwerp, where he lived with an archaeologist and became an assistant to a historical painter. In 1864 he moved to Paris, where he worked until emigrating to London after the outbreak of the Franco-Prussian War in 1870. In England he incorporated his middle name into his surname to give himself an alphabetical advantage at exhibitions, and changed Laurens to Lawrence. His popularity grew steadily and his work soon commanded top prices, among the highest of any artist active at the time. England remained his home, and in 1899 he was knighted by Queen Victoria. From the 1890s until his death in 1912, he was a mainstay of social and artistic life of London.

By far the largest painting Alma-Tadema ever produced, *Spring* is a magnificent demonstration of the contradictory aspirations toward veracity and idealization that characterize Victorian painting. Alma-Tadema carefully researched the archaeological details of his pictures. He was an expert on the appearance of the many kinds of marble and used photographs of classical sites and artifacts to upgrade his accuracy. In *Spring,* Alma-Tadema illustrates a celebration such as the Cerealia, the Roman festival dedicated to Ceres, the goddess of fertility and crops. The buildings are accurate composites of Roman architecture; the inscription on the arch in the middle of the background is from Trajan's Arch at Benevento, and the frieze with the centaurs approximates a Greek relief in the British Museum.

All this research, however, was accumulated to serve the same vision of classical perfection that is invoked by Algernon Swinburne's verse inscribed at the bottom of the picture frame:

> In a land of clear colours and stories
> In a region of shadowless hours,
> Where earth has a garment of glories
> And a murmur of musical flowers.

Ca. 1895; Oil on canvas; 70¼ × 31½ inches

Jean Léon Gérôme
Pollice Verso

PHOENIX ART MUSEUM

Although Jean Léon Gérôme (1824–1904) is remembered as the academician who denounced Impressionism as "the dishonor of French art," he was esteemed during his lifetime for respecting the diverse talents of his pupils, among them Thomas Eakins and Fernand Léger. Gérôme was a pupil of history painter Paul Delaroche, whom he accompanied to Rome in 1844. There Gérôme copied classical artifacts and became a learned amateur archaeologist. Typical of his early works were semierotic genre scenes in antique settings; later he expanded his repertoire to include large-scale historical allegories.

As a realist history painter, Gérôme created carefully researched, archaeologically correct pictures composed as if the artist had been present when the events occurred. Before painting *Pollice Verso,* for example, Gérôme spent the equivalent of $3,000 to obtain casts of authentic gladiator helmets and buckles which he had coated in metal before outfitting his model.

Pollice Verso illustrates the moment when the outcome of a Roman gladiatorial contest is being decided by the audience's turning of thumbs. Gérôme gives us a view of the Colosseum from the arena floor, providing both a detailed close-up of the combatants and a wide-angle panorama of the sanguineous crowd. The most ferocious spectators are the Vestal Virgins in their luxuriously appointed box to the left of the emperor, who gauges the temper of the crowd. The details are marvelously painted, especially the bands of light shining through unseen stretches of awning, the banners, the rugs, and the armor of the gladiators.

The accuracy of Gérôme's painting became the subject of considerable debate. It is not known whether the Roman sign of disfavor, *pollice verso* (literally "turned thumb"), actually meant "thumbs up" or "thumbs down." Alexander T. Stewart, the American dry-goods magnate and former classics teacher who bought *Pollice Verso* from Gérôme, published a pamphlet of rather ambiguous excerpts from ancient sources to prove that Gérôme's interpretation was correct. Correct or not, thanks to the popularity of the picture, Gérôme's interpretation won out. Since 1874, *pollice verso* has meant "thumbs down."

1874; Oil on canvas; 39½ × 58⅛ inches

Lysippos (?)
The Getty Bronze

THE J. PAUL GETTY MUSEUM
MALIBU, CALIFORNIA

On the seabed near the port of Fano, an Italian fisherman found what many experts believe to be the only surviving work by Lysippos (fourth century B.C.), court sculptor to Alexander the Great. The bronze figure was discovered in 1963, encased in a thick layer of encrustation built up over centuries of immersion in the Adriatic. It was later acquired by Artemis, the Luxembourg-based art consortium, which supervised its restoration. In the early 1970s, photographs of the bronze were sent to J. Paul Getty, whose plan for his new museum was in its final stages. Negotiations were begun in 1972, but it was not until 1977, a year after Getty's death, that the museum was able to acquire the bronze.

Conservators discovered that the figure was constructed over an armature of reed sticks covered with a solid mixture of pebbles, ivory fragments, pottery shards, pistachio nut shells, and glue. The main outlines were shaped in clay, and the final modeling was done on wax sheets applied to the surface of the figure. The sculpture was then cast in golden yellow bronze; copper nipples and lips were added, and glass and crystal eyes fringed with finely cut bronze eyelashes were set in the eye sockets.

The statue represents a very young man. The olive leaves with which he is crowned signify victory in the Olympic Games, and there is evidence that the left hand originally held a palm branch, another attribute of the athletic victor. In contrast to the impersonal idealization characteristic of earlier Greek statuary, *The Getty Bronze* is distinguished by its subtle individuation—finely chiseled hair, delicate wrists, long, thin, upturned fingers, dimpled chin, and bowed, sensual lips. The self-confident pose suggests that the young man was not meant to be perceived as an ordinary mortal.

Lysippos had a long and active career. He worked exclusively in bronze and was renowned as a portraitist; it was said that Alexander the Great refused to have his image modeled by anyone else.

Lysippos was also celebrated for creating sculpture with "soul"; *The Getty Bronze* is particularly distinguished by its psychological presence. The sculpture "achieves the miracle that the viewer feels unity with the subject," says Getty Museum Curator of Antiquities Jiří Frel. "You yourself won at Olympia and share all the vertigo of it."

Fourth century B.C.; Bronze; height 59½ inches

Auguste Rodin
The Thinker

THE BALTIMORE MUSEUM OF ART

In 1880, the French government commissioned Auguste Rodin (1840–1917) to create a bronze portal with sculpted decoration based on Dante's *The Divine Comedy*. The doors, known as *The Gates of Hell,* became the great effort of Rodin's life. The project functioned as a source of inspiration for hundreds of figures, several of which later became famous when he enlarged them as independent works. The best known of these enlargements, *The Thinker* was originally designed to occupy a projection above the center of the lintel, where it served as the compositional and psychological focus of the doors.

Who is *The Thinker?* Judith Cladel, Rodin's biographer, writes that the name was first given to the figure by foundry workers who saw its resemblance to Michelangelo's statue of Lorenzo de' Medici, also called *The Thinker.* When Rodin first exhibited the figure in 1889, it was entitled *The Poet,* and most interpreters presumed that it represented Dante, meditating upon his poem. In an interview published in 1904, however, Rodin gave another interpretation: "*The Thinker* has a story. In days long gone by, I conceived the idea of *The Gates of Hell.* Before the door, seated on a rock, Dante, thinking of the plan of his poem. Behind him, Ugolino, Francesca, Paolo, all the characters of *The Divine Comedy.* . . . Thin, ascetic Dante separated from the whole would have been without meaning. Guided by my first inspiration I conceived another thinker, a naked man, seated upon a rock, his feet drawn under him, his fist against his teeth, he dreams. The fertile thought slowly elaborates itself within his brain. He is no longer dreamer, he is creator." Rodin's thinker, therefore, is a personification of the creative artist and, in fact, it was Rodin's wish that a cast of *The Thinker* serve as his own grave marker.

Enlarged and exhibited independently, *The Thinker* has always been widely admired. Cast under the artist's supervision, the Baltimore Museum's *Thinker* is the earliest example of the enlarged series. Its prominence within the Baltimore collection attests to Rodin's ability to formulate a powerful, universal image, whose symbolism, according to the museum, is a "source of never-failing interest and can never be worn out."

1880; Bronze; 79 inches
The Jacob Epstein Collection

Decorative Arts
and Textiles

Peter Carl Fabergé
Imperial Easter Egg

VIRGINIA MUSEUM · RICHMOND

One of the most inventive jewelry designers in the history of Western decorative arts, Russian artist Peter Carl Fabergé (1846–1920) gained worldwide renown for creating exquisite and ingenious objects of fantasy—animals, figure groups, bibelots, flowers, and above all jeweled Easter eggs, especially prized by European royalty. The ceremonial presentation of elaborately decorated Easter eggs originated in the eighteenth century in the court of Versailles, where Boucher and Watteau were among the artists who painted eggshells. Sometime in 1884 Fabergé persuaded Tsar Alexander III to commission a similar Easter gift for the Tsarina Maria Feodorovna, to be executed in precious stones and to contain a "surprise." Pleased with the results, the tsar made the commission an annual tradition. His son Nicholas II, who vowed "to follow my father in everything," continued the tradition for both the dowager empress and his wife, Tsarina Alexandra.

Of the fifty-eight eggs Fabergé fashioned for the tsar and his family, forty-five are known to survive, five in the collection of the Virginia Museum. The rock crystal egg, the earliest of the Virginia group, is encircled with a gold diamond-set band and stands on a gold and enamel base ornamented with diamond-outlined monograms of Tsarina Alexandra. A gold shaft topped with a Siberian cabochon emerald extends through the center of the egg. Pressing down on the emerald lowers a hook that engages the miniature paintings inside the globe, causing them to revolve. Each painting depicts a royal residence connected with the life of Tsarina Alexandra up to the time of the egg's presentation in 1896, among them Rosenau in Coberg, where she became engaged; the Winter Palace, site of her wedding in 1894; Anitchkov Palace, the newlyweds' first residence; and Windsor Castle, where the tsarina traveled to visit her grandmother, Queen Victoria.

The Russian Revolution of 1917 abruptly ended Fabergé's Easter commissions; the new government officially denounced such objects of luxury and Fabergé died in exile in 1920.

Ca. 1896; Precious stones, gold, rock crystal, enamel; 10 × 4 inches
Bequest from the Estate of Lillian Thomas Pratt

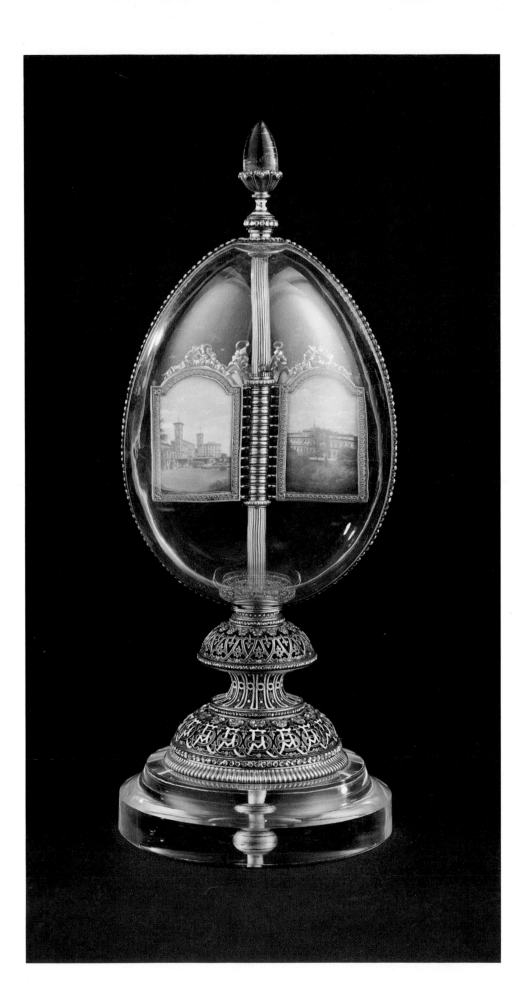

Artist Unknown
Libation Dish of Darius the Great

CINCINNATI ART MUSEUM

A legendary king, Achaemenes, founded a dynasty of Persian rulers in the ninth century B.C. By the time of Darius the Great, who ruled from 521 to 486 B.C., the Achaemenid dynasty ruled all of Persia and large sections of northern India. This new access to authority prompted the creation of unprecedented forms of imperial art, ranging from Darius's magnificent palace at Persepolis to gold and silver drinking vessels embellished with native designs.

The gold Achaemenid libation dish at the Cincinnati Art Museum is inscribed "Darius Great King" on the back of the rim in cuneiform characters of Old Persian, Elamite, and Neo-Babylonian, the three languages of Darius's kingdom. When the vessel is filled with red wine, its design suggests a cross-section of a pomegranate, the fruit from which a favored wine was made.

Darius standardized coinage, weights, and measurements, and a notable feature of Cincinnati's ceremonial dish is that it holds exactly one liter of liquid. Although it has been suggested that the high quality of such golden vessels is attributable to the large-scale importation of Greek craftsmen under Darius, recent excavations indicate that delicate, skillfully crafted metalwork had already been a native tradition in Persia for centuries.

522–485 B.C.; Gold; 12 inches in diameter

Honami Koetsu and Tawaraya Sotatsu
Hand Scroll of Deer and Poems

SEATTLE ART MUSEUM

Honami Koetsu and Tawaraya Sotatsu were both born in the latter half of the sixteenth century, when a powerful class of merchant bankers shaped the economic, political, and cultural development of Japan. As patrons, the merchants supported a revival of the classic culture of the Heian period, remembered in such prose masterpieces as *Tale of Genji* and *Tale of Ise*. For Koetsu and Sotatsu, the Heian period (794–1185) provided an ideal of refinement, and both artists dedicated themselves to furthering these classical concepts of elegance and beauty.

Koetsu (1558–1637), born to a distinguished family of connoisseurs and sword makers, was Japan's great renaissance man. Calligrapher, potter, tea master, lacquerist, master of Nō drama, he celebrated tradition with luxurious new decorative forms. In 1615 the warlord Tokugawa Ieyasu presented Koetsu with a land grant at Takagamine, north of Kyoto, where Koetsu established an artists' community and produced much of the calligraphy and ceramics for which he was especially famous.

It is thought that Sotatsu (1576–1643) also belonged to the wealthy Kyoto merchant class. Sotatsu presided over Tawaraya, a renowned Kyoto painting and fan-making establishment. Emphasizing graceful line, refined proportions, and a balanced distribution of rich colors rather than representational qualities, Sotatsu was particularly adept at creating compositions for variously shaped surfaces—screens, hand scrolls, sliding door panels, and fans.

Sotatsu and Koetsu met about 1605 when both men were mature artists. Together they excelled in the creation of hand scrolls that unite literature, calligraphy, and decorative painting in a single work of art. In the deer scroll, Koetsu's calligraphy is ideally suited to its poetry from the *Shin Kokinshu*, an anthology of ancient and modern poetic works compiled in the thirteenth century. Composed in variously weighted inks from the heaviest black to the palest gray, the calligraphy corresponds in transparency and opacity to the washes employed for the animal forms. Koetsu's writing overlays Sotatsu's figurative designs, freely brushed in gold and silver to catch the light, creating shifts in spatial effects. The deer, symbols of autumn, set the mood as well as the pace for the reading of the poems with their movements around, above, and below the verses.

Detail; Early seventeenth century; Ink, gold, and silver on paper; 12½ inches × 30 feet 3¾ inches
Gift of Mrs. Donald E. Frederick

Artist Unknown
Tibetan Temple Hanging

LOS ANGELES COUNTY MUSEUM OF ART

Buddhism was introduced in Tibet in the seventh century and by the mid-eighth century began to replace Bon, the country's native shamanistic religion. In the fifteenth century the belief arose that abbots of certain Buddhist monasteries were incarnations of the Compassionate Buddha Avalokitesvara, the patron saint of Tibet. These abbots are the Dalai Lamas, who served as the theocratic rulers of Tibet until 1959. The Los Angeles County Museum's temple hanging was a gift for the present Dalai Lama's summer palace at Norbulinga in Central Tibet and was presented to commemorate his enthronement at age five in 1940.

Made for religious festivals, this appliquéd and brocaded silk panel depicts celestial or self-born Buddhas encircled by mandalas and stylized lotus blossoms. In 1959 the People's Republic of China, which has occupied Tibet since 1950, began a program of religious suppression which forced the Dalai Lama into exile and resulted in the destruction of many temples and religious artifacts. A few paintings and ritual fabrics subsequently found their way into foreign collections, among them Los Angeles's exceptionally colorful and well-crafted temple hanging.

Detail; 1940; Colored silk; 67 × 40 inches
Gift of Mr. and Mrs. James Coburn

Artist Unknown
The Unicorn in Captivity

THE CLOISTERS · METROPOLITAN MUSEUM OF ART · NEW YORK CITY

Scholars and public alike often rank them as the most magnificent tapestries in existence, but no one knows who commissioned the Unicorn tapestries or for what occasion they were produced. The seven panels were probably woven in Brussels around 1500, but nothing is certain about their history until 1681, when the tapestries are mentioned in an inventory of Duke François de la Rochefoucard's possessions. During the French Revolution, the panels were seized from the Rochefoucard château outside Paris and were used for several decades to cover peasants' fruit trees and vegetables against frost. In the 1850s, after Count Hippolyte de la Rochefoucard heard about some "old curtains" stored in a barn, the tapestries were hung again in the family château.

The tapestries, in excellent condition despite their misuse, illustrate the medieval legend that a unicorn could only be captured by a virgin. On an allegorical level, the unicorn symbolized Christ reincarnate as well as a lover-bridegroom; the virgin, the Virgin Mary. The legend was also interpreted as an allegory of courtly love, suggesting that the tapestries may have been woven as a wedding gift.

The best-known of the tapestries is the seventh, depicting a unicorn enclosed by a fence. The animal is leashed with a golden chain, a symbol of marriage, to a tree bearing pomegranates, symbolic of Christ, immortality, and human fertility; what appears to be blood on the unicorn's body is juice dripping from the fruit above. The wild orchid silhouetted against the animal's body was believed an aphrodisiac. At the animal's right foreleg is the bistort, an aid to fertility. The Madonna lily in the right foreground, reputedly the lily of the Song of Songs, symbolizes the purity of the Virgin and faithfulness in love and marriage. The green frog to the right of the lily was reported to have an aphrodisiac bone in its left side.

The Unicorn tapestries came to the Cloisters, the Metropolitan Museum's medieval branch, in 1937, since when their charm and vivacity have continually ranked them among the museum's most admired possessions.

Ca. 1500; Wool and silk with metal threads; 12 feet 1 inch × 8 feet 3 inches
Gift of John D. Rockefeller, Jr., The Cloisters Collection, 1937

Artist Unknown
Prayer Rug with Three Arches

THE TEXTILE MUSEUM · WASHINGTON, D.C.

Carpets woven for the Ottoman sultans of Turkey in the sixteenth and seventeenth centuries are among the most handsome ever produced. Dating from the end of this period, the Textile Museum's *Prayer Rug with Three Arches* is based on earlier prototypes woven in the Istanbul area for the sultans. This style was adapted by Anatolian village weavers, who probably wove the rug to conform with their own aesthetic preference for bold colors and angular patterns.

As in all prayer rugs, the design relates to religious function. Because it must be carried, the rug is relatively small. The central field contains a mihrab, or prayer niche, corresponding to the prayer niche in the wall of a mosque. The mihrab marks the place of the worshiper on the rug, who points the apex toward Mecca. The triple arches with a higher central unit, a Roman triumphal architectural form adopted by the Muslims for their palaces and mosques, first appear on carpets in the late sixteenth century. Dating of Ottoman carpets has been greatly assisted by their appearance in seventeenth-century Netherlandish paintings; a still life canvas by Nicholaes van Gelder painted in 1664, for example, shows a carpet with capitals, columns, leaf-decorated spandrels, and border that closely resemble those of the Textile Museum's *Prayer Rug with Three Arches*.

Late seventeenth or early eighteenth century; Wool; 5 feet 6 inches × 3 feet 8 inches
Gift of Heinrich Jacoby

Artist Unknown
Quilled Buckskin Shirt

GLENBOW MUSEUM · CALGARY, ALBERTA

The Blackfoot Indians once controlled territory extending from northern Saskatchewan to the southernmost headwaters of the Missouri River. For the first quarter of the nineteenth century the Blackfeet forcibly prevented the white man from expanding the lucrative beaver-trapping trade to the upper tributaries of the Missouri. Even after signing treaties with the United States, the Blackfeet continued to wear—and still wear—warrior shirts as symbols of their honor and prestige.

The Glenbow Museum is especially noted for its wide range of Blackfoot artifacts, none more impressive than this elaborately decorated warrior's shirt, exceptional in its quality of workmanship and striking colors. The garment is fashioned from painted buckskin and ornamented with feathers, trade bells, scalp locks, and porcupine quills arranged in a typically Blackfoot V-shaped design over the shoulders and bodice. The shirt terminates in very long fringe, a decorative element whose difficulty of execution is proportional to length. To complete the costume a warrior would probably have added leggings, moccasins, a rawhide-bound hairbone breastplate, and perhaps a headdress consisting of a few feathers pointing straight up. Such ensembles were not worn in active combat but were reserved for camp ceremonies and donned for visiting dignitaries.

Late nineteenth century; Buckskin, feathers, quills, scalp locks, bells; length approximately 42 inches

Artist Unknown
Kansas Crib Quilt

THE MUSEUM OF AMERICAN FOLK ART · NEW YORK CITY

Quilts have brought more people to folk art than any other kind of artifact, according to the staff of the Museum of American Folk Art. Quilts are part of the pastoral legend of the American homestead, boldly declaring the inventiveness and manual skill of ordinary female citizens. Intuitively manipulating geometric forms, these women transformed pieced quilts into a medium for expressing their personal interests, the histories of their families, and the politics and progress of America. Names of traditional quilt-making patterns indicate wide-ranging sources of inspiration—architecture (Gothic Windows, Courthouse Steps, Log Cabin); religion (Jacob's Ladder, World Without End, Star of Bethlehem); politics (Kansas Troubles, Lincoln's Platform, Jackson Star); nature (Bear's Paw, Fly Foot, North Carolina Lily); historical events (Underground Railway, Free Trade Patch, Nelson's Victory); common objects (Indian Hatchet, Monkey Wrench, Hour Glass).

Baby quilts represent a distinctive quilt-making genre. While their primary function was to provide warmth in a cradle or crib, they were also placed on the floor as colorful padding for infants too young to crawl. Most were probably sewn by mothers-to-be, but older children often learned to master quilt making by sewing bedcovers for their dolls and newborn brothers and sisters.

The unknown creator of this Kansas baby quilt pieced together hand-dyed homespun cotton into a striped field embellished with an appliquéd central star. The smaller white stars and the word "baby" are embroidered in white thread. It is sometimes possible to date quilts with patriotic designs on the basis of the number of stars they feature. In this case the blue center star contains thirty-four smaller stars: in 1861 Kansas became the thirty-fourth state, a fact which may not only establish the quilt's age but also provide a double meaning for the word "baby."

Ca. 1861; Homespun cotton; 36 × 36¼ inches
Collection of Phyllis Haders

Impressionism and Post-Impressionism

Claude Monet
Boulevard des Capucines

THE NELSON-ATKINS MUSEUM OF ART · KANSAS CITY, MISSOURI

Boulevard des Capucines illustrates the view from the second-story window of Parisian photographer Nadar's studio, where the first Impressionist exhibition was held in 1874. The location prompted Edgar Degas to suggest that the group call itself La Capucine ("nasturtium") and that the flower be included on posters announcing the exhibition. Instead the group came to be known by the derisive term "Impressionist" used to describe their paintings in a satirical review in the Parisian journal *Charivari*.

Boulevard des Capucines, by Claude Monet (1840–1926), was one of the paintings *Charivari* singled out for ridicule. In the review a fictitious academic painter stands before the painting and begins to lose his reason. "Now there's impressionism, or I don't know what it means," the painter says. "Will you only be so good as to tell me what those innumerable tongue-lickings in the lower part of the picture represent?"

"Why those are people walking along," his companion replies.

"Then do I look like that when I am walking along the boulevard? Blood and thunder! So you are making fun of me at last." The conservative painter begins dancing about in front of the picture singing, "Hi-ho, I am impressionism on the march, the avenging palette knife, the *Boulevard des Capucines* of Monet. . . ."

Regarded today as one of the most atmospherically subtle and perceptive of Monet's pictures, *Boulevard des Capucines* has been compared to Paris street scene photographs of the 1860s and 1870s. These photographs frequently contain blurred images of moving pedestrians not unlike the "tongue-lickings" on Monet's canvas. The influence of photography on Monet's representations of motion is a matter of conjecture, but it may not be inconsequential that a leading Paris photographer loaned the painter his premises to paint two versions of *Boulevard des Capucines*.

1873–74; Oil on canvas; 31¼ × 23¼ inches
Acquired through the Kenneth A. and Helen F. Spencer Foundation Acquisition Fund

Claude Monet
Springtime

THE WALTERS ART GALLERY
BALTIMORE, MARYLAND

"The word 'Impressionism' was created for him and fits him better than it does anyone else," said critic Felix Fénéon of Claude Monet (1840–1926). Monet took his initial steps toward Impressionism at the age of eighteen after meeting Eugène Boudin. Boudin was one of the first French landscape painters to move out of his studio and paint outdoors, directly from nature. "Everything that is painted directly on the spot," Boudin believed, "has always a strength, a power, a vividness of touch that one doesn't find again in the studio." This observation launched Monet's search for a new method of capturing the changing effects of sunlight he experienced as he painted outdoor scenes. From recent scientific studies he learned that color was not an inherent property of an object but rather a function of the light reflected from it: together with his ambition to capture transient atmospheric effects, this revelation ultimately produced a technique which interprets all visual reality in terms of light.

From 1872 to 1875 Monet lived primarily at Argenteuil, on the Seine near Paris, where he was joined by his colleagues Auguste Renoir and Edouard Manet. There Monet painted his wife, Camille, and their son, as did Renoir and Manet. *Springtime,* also titled *Camille Reading,* is variously dated within this period.

Figures in a garden or outdoor setting were among Monet's frequent subjects as he developed his Impressionist style. In his Argenteuil paintings, the emphasis begins to shift from the figure to the landscape. There is a hint of this transition in *Springtime,* where the model is bathed in reflections from surrounding blossoms. By placing her under overhanging foliage, Monet was able to address the special problem of light falling through the branches. The skirt, in addition to its role as costume, serves as a field for investigating the effects of dappled sunshine. The figure, nevertheless, remains the dominant element. Rendered naturalistically, without allegorical gestures or trappings, she represents an Impressionist vision of the ideal modern woman.

Ca. 1872; Oil on canvas; 19⅛ × 25¼ inches

Claude Monet
Water Lilies

THE PORTLAND ART MUSEUM
PORTLAND, OREGON

In 1890, Claude Monet (1840–1926) acquired a strip of marshland across the road from his house at Giverny, fifty-two miles north of Paris. A tributary of the Epte River flowed through the property; by diverting the stream he was able to construct the water lily garden, now a French national monument, that inspired his famed series of lily paintings.

Monet later revealed to the critic Louis Guillemot his ambition to create an ensemble of water landscapes for a self-contained architectural space. "One imagines a circular room," Guillemot recounted, "the walls of which, above the baseboard, would be entirely filled with water [paintings] dotted with plants to the very horizon. . . ." Although several attempts were made to realize the project during Monet's lifetime, it was not until after his death in 1926 that some of his canvases were placed as he envisioned them, in two eighty-foot oval rooms at the Orangerie museum in Paris.

A snapshot taken July 8, 1915, shows seventy-four-year-old Monet seated under a large umbrella painting the canvas now in the Portland Art Museum. He was suffering from cataracts on both eyes and found his vision most accurate in the mornings and evenings when the pond's surface contrasted most vividly with the blossoms. Under these conditions he was able to produce a number of large, broadly rendered studies of the pond surface typified by the Portland canvas. Georges Clemenceau, the statesman and journalist who was the painter's close friend, described Monet at work under his umbrella: "For hours he would stay there without moving, voiceless in his armchair, searching with his glance, seeking to read in their reflections the hidden nature of things. The water drank in the light and transposed it, sublimated it to its quintessence before returning it to the sensitive retina surprised by unknown reactions. Rightly speaking, it is therein that lies the miracle of the *Water Lilies,* which show us the order of things as other than we had observed it so far."

1915; Oil on canvas; 63¾ × 71⅛ inches
Helen Thurston Ayer Fund

Camille Pissarro
Near Sydenham Hill

KIMBELL ART MUSEUM
FORT WORTH, TEXAS

Of all the Impressionists, Camille Pissarro (1830–1903) felt most at home in England. His first stay was occasioned by the Franco-Prussian War: like Claude Monet, Pissarro fled to London before Paris fell to the Germans in 1870, remaining there until after the armistice in 1871. Pissarro later recalled, "Monet and I were very enthusiastic over the London landscapes. Monet worked in the parks whilst I, living in lower Norwood, at that time a charming suburb, studied the effect of fog, snow and springtime."

Near Sydenham Hill, painted on location, illustrates the results of this study. In the picture's middle distance is the village of lower Norwood, separated from the foreground fields by the suburban rail line to London. Color harmonies are keyed to the damp, silvery mist that envelops the distant hills and establishes the proximity of the trees and fence. Atmosphere, temperature, and weather are the subjects of this painting, much as in the paintings being done then by Monet. Pissarro, however, was less inclined than Monet to explore atmospheric effects that resulted in a breakdown of physical contours, and always retained a respect for the material facts of his subject matter.

Reflecting on these years in England, Pissarro preferred to remember his enthusiasm for London landscapes rather than events in France. Returning home, he found his house looted and nearly all his work from the first fifteen years of his career destroyed by Prussian soldiers who had used his canvases to wipe their shoes.

Revered for his patience, kindness, and wisdom —"a man to consult and something like the good Lord" in Cézanne's estimation—Pissarro was later ranked as a second-string Impressionist. Recent reevaluations of his work are changing this assessment: While less facile and flamboyant than some of his younger associates, Pissarro was very often more profound.

1871; Oil on canvas; 17 × 21 inches

Edgar Degas
Portrait of Estelle Musson

NEW ORLEANS MUSEUM OF ART

In October 1872, Edgar Degas (1834–1917) arrived in New Orleans for a five-month visit. New Orleans was the birthplace of his mother, Marie-Célestine Musson, the home of his uncle, Michel Musson, and the site of a wine-importing business established four years earlier by his younger brothers, René and Achille. Most of the family lived together in Michel Musson's mansion at 372 Esplanade, one of the city's most elegant avenues, and Degas moved in with them for the duration of his stay.

Degas's brother René lived in the family mansion with his wife, Estelle, who was Michel Musson's daughter and hence first cousin to both the artist and her own husband. Estelle had been previously married to a captain in the Confederate army who was killed nine months after the wedding, at the Battle of Corinth. Three weeks after his death, in October 1862, the couple's daughter was born. Early the following year, the infant and her mother, grandmother, and aunt sailed to Europe, where they visited the Degas family in Paris and Italy. Greatly impressed by his widowed cousin, René Degas accompanied the women back to New Orleans after the defeat of the Confederacy in 1865. The following year René returned to Paris to arrange financing for the business he intended to establish in America. During his absence Estelle was suddenly stricken with ophthalmia and became totally blind. The couple was married nevertheless in 1868.

Edgar Degas admired his blind sister-in-law and painted three portraits of her during his visit. This one, which shows Estelle anchored against a table and arranging flowers through a delicate sense of touch, came up for auction in 1964. According to Charles Mo, former senior curator at the New Orleans Museum of Art, "because the painting recalls Degas's visit to New Orleans, it caught the public's imagination. Funds were raised by public subscription . . . from all sectors of the populace."

1872; Oil on canvas; 39¾ × 53¹⁵/₁₆ inches
Photograph: Roy Trahan, New Orleans, Louisiana

Gustave Caillebotte
The Streets of Paris on a Rainy Day

THE ART INSTITUTE OF CHICAGO

Largely forgotten by the time of the artist's death, *The Streets of Paris on a Rainy Day* by Gustave Caillebotte (1849–1894) was among the most-discussed canvases at the third Impressionist exhibition in Paris in 1877. Twenty-eight-year-old Caillebotte was then at the height of his career, both as a painter and as a leader of the Impressionist movement. A member of a prominent Parisian banking family, Caillebotte studied at the École des Beaux-Arts. In 1873, he inherited a large fortune and began buying Impressionist paintings.

Until recently, Caillebotte was better known as a patron than as a painter. Like others in the Impressionist group, Caillebotte painted transient moments in everyday life, often presented as segments of a larger continuum. But his palette was too subdued, his focus was too sharp, and his compositions were too calculated to fit the typical model of Impressionist style. *Rainy Day* suggests a further departure. Its setting is a section of Paris completely rebuilt in Caillebotte's lifetime by Baron Georges Haussmann, city planner under Napoleon III. Eliminating crooked streets and irregular, semimedieval construction, Haussmann enhanced the city's commercial access and military security with a system of broad boulevards and uniformly scaled architecture. Caillebotte's painting accurately depicts the new, modern city and hints of its psychological environment as well. Preoccupied and isolated under their umbrellas, the fashionable strollers are physically or mentally remote from one another, afflicted, perhaps, with a touch of ennui. It is this psychological complexity that most distinguishes *Rainy Day* and may elevate Caillebotte's fame as a prescient observer of modern urban life.

1877; Oil on canvas; 83¼ × 118½ inches
Charles H. and Mary F. S. Worcester Collection

Auguste Renoir
Romaine Lacaux

THE CLEVELAND MUSEUM OF ART

Auguste Renoir (1841–1919) was twenty-three years old when he painted *Romaine Lacaux,* the first of his many portraits of children. He had recently completed his final examinations at the École des Beaux-Arts, where his comrades were Frédéric Bazille, Claude Monet, and Alfred Sisley. His friends encouraged him to continue his work. But lacking income or patrons, Renoir was tempted to resume his former occupations of china painting and decorating window shades to look like stained-glass windows for French missionaries in Africa.

Renoir decided instead to visit the forest of Fontainebleau, leaving behind for consideration by the 1864 Salon jury *La Esmeralda,* a large nocturnal scene inspired by a Victor Hugo story, *The Hunchback of Notre Dame.* In Fontainebleau, Renoir met by chance the painter Narcisse Diaz de la Peña, whose work he very much admired. Diaz, acknowledging the younger painter's talent, admonished him at the same time for his dark, academic palette. This trip provided the turning point in Renoir's career: during his visit *La Esmeralda* was accepted for exhibition at the 1864 Salon, a great triumph for a young unknown painter. Returning from Fontainebleau after the exhibition, Renoir destroyed the canvas, vowing never again to be associated with a painting distinguished by large masses of black.

Painted the same year he created and destroyed his first successful Salon picture, Renoir's *Romaine Lacaux* is the work of an innovator barely inhibited by tradition. Mademoiselle Lacaux was the daughter of a judge known for his fervent admiration of the composer Richard Wagner. Judge Lacaux is thought to have commissioned the portrait while his family was on holiday in Fontainebleau at the time of Renoir's visit. It is one of the earliest surviving canvases by Renoir, who destroyed many of his paintings from the early to mid 1860s, and it is unquestionably the most successful of the early group. The influence of Corot, Couture, Ingres, and society portraitist Franz Winterhalter has been detected in the compositional form and silver-toned palette, while the background flowers presage the Impressionist technique Renoir developed with Monet five years later. In this case, Renoir's stylistic precursors are not so much imitated as adapted to serve his particular instinct for delicacy and refinement: the subdued, close-valued color scheme, reminiscent of Corot, conveys an atmosphere of gentleness while the straightforward Ingres-like pose moves the painting away from sentimentality by emphasizing the child's alert, intelligent expression. Although Renoir had not yet found his distinctive personal style, *Romaine Lacaux* provides objective evidence of the extraordinary skill that led to its development.

1864; Oil on canvas, 31⅞ × 25½ inches
Gift of Hanna Fund

Auguste Renoir
A Girl with a Watering Can

NATIONAL GALLERY OF ART · WASHINGTON, D.C.

The painter Edgar Degas once observed that his friend Auguste Renoir (1841–1919) "played with color like a kitten playing with a ball of colored wool." This uninhibited fascination with the sensations of color is evident in *A Girl with a Watering Can,* painted when Renoir was at the height of his enthusiasm for Impressionist technique. Renoir adopted a small, comma-shaped brushstroke, recreating forms rather than defining them through intricate juxtapositions of pure pigment. In *A Girl with a Watering Can* this web of prismatic brushwork merges the child's form with those of the foliage and unifies the painting's surface in a scintillating shimmer. Particular attention has been paid to the manner in which sunlight is absorbed by different textures; the gravel path sparkles while the child's skin radiates a luminous glow.

The painting presents the viewpoint of a child: the landscape is depicted from the girl's level of vision, and her watering can suggests a proprietary claim, even if imaginary, on the surrounding garden. Above all, the composition projects a sense of childish delight in the colorful pleasures of a superb summer day. The flower tender's identity is unknown, although a dealer who purchased the painting in 1898 from its owner, Count Batthiany, was told that it represented the count's wife, Sellière, when she was five years old.

1876; Oil on canvas; 39½ × 28¾ inches
Chester Dale Collection

Auguste Renoir
The Dance at Bougival

MUSEUM OF FINE ARTS · BOSTON, MASSACHUSETTS

At the request of his dealer, Auguste Renoir (1841–1919) began work in the autumn of 1892 on two paintings on the theme of the dance, one set in the city and the other, *The Dance at Bougival,* in the country. For the city version Renoir's models were his future wife, Aline Charigot, and the painter Paul Lhote; for the country canvas he coupled the male dancer with an eighteen-year-old Montmartre model, Maria-Clémentine, later known as an artist in her own right by her pseudonym, Suzanne Valadon.

Valadon typified the Montmartre model: she was sturdy, bursting with health, graceful, seductive, lighthearted, and extroverted. Toulouse-Lautrec painted her portrait as did Puvis de Chavannes who introduced her to Renoir. Renoir painted her several times, apparently much to the displeasure of Aline Charigot.

"I am the dancer who smiles as she falls into the arms of her partner," said Valadon of *Dance at Bougival.* Renoir framed her face in a red bonnet to create the focal point of the composition, a device underscored by the hidden but amorous gaze of her companion. The setting conforms to the description of the Fournaise restaurant at Bougival provided some years later by Renoir's son Jean: "The place was delightful; a perpetual holiday. . . . At night there was always someone who volunteered to play the piano. The tables on the terrace were pushed back into the corner. The piano was in a little reception room and the music floated out through an open window."

1883; Oil on canvas; 70 × 38 inches
Purchased, Picture Fund

Auguste Renoir
Mother and Child

CALIFORNIA PALACE OF THE LEGION OF HONOR · SAN FRANCISCO

The property of a private German collector since 1909, *Mother and Child* by Auguste Renoir (1841–1919) made headlines when it was rediscovered and sold to the California Palace of the Legion of Honor in 1951. On the basis of the broad, sketchy style and the facial features of the woman, the subjects were first identified as the artist's son Claude, born in 1901, and Gabrielle Renard, a cousin of Madame Renoir who served as the family nursemaid and became one of Renoir's most famous late models. Then Renard, married and living in Los Angeles when the painting was rediscovered, emphatically disclaimed it as a portrait of Claude and herself. Now the child is identified as Claude's older brother, Jean, the great French filmmaker, who was born in 1894.

Jean Renoir remembered, "One of the most striking characteristics of my father and his household was their reserve. They all had an instinctive aversion to any conspicuous display of personal emotions. Renoir would have given his life for his children without hesitation. But he was extremely reticent about revealing his private feelings to anyone—even perhaps to himself. When he was seated at his easel it was a different story. There he no longer felt any restraint. With sharp but tender touches of the brush he would joyfully caress the dimples in the cheek or the little creases in the wrist of his children, and shout his love to the universe."

Rough outlines of three figures in the painting's background indicate that Renoir originally had a more elaborate composition in mind, but since the picture remained unsold until some years after it was painted it is unlikely that the work is unintentionally unfinished. The painting is not varnished, a rarity in Renoir's case, which contributes to its unusual transparency and delicacy of tone. A year after its acquisition, the California Palace of the Legion of Honor noted that "the people of this community have so completely taken it to their hearts that it has already become a pilgrimage picture."

Ca. 1895; Oil on canvas; 46 × 41 inches
Mildred Anna Williams Fund

Auguste Renoir
The Luncheon of the Boating Party

THE PHILLIPS COLLECTION
WASHINGTON, D.C.

The Luncheon of the Boating Party marks a major turning point in Auguste Renoir's (1841–1919) career. Shortly after its completion he traveled to Italy, where his study of Renaissance classicism deepened his dissatisfaction with the amorphous contours of Impressionist brushwork and convinced him that "in a word, I was at a dead end." A suggestion of this dissatisfaction may be gleaned from the relative solidity of forms in *Luncheon,* but the mood and the brilliant colors link it unequivocally with Impressionism.

The painting was executed at the terrace of the Fournaise restaurant at Bougival, a favorite gathering place for the artist and his friends on the Seine, near Paris. There is some disagreement about who is depicted, but most historians agree that the man seated backwards in the chair is the engineer and painter Gustave Caillebotte (page 67). On his right is Renoir's model Angèle, who appears again in the background, drinking. In the right corner, wearing a straw hat, is the art historian and banker Charles Ephrussi. There is no dispute about the name of the almond-eyed woman at the left playing with the dog: she is Aline Charigot, a young native of Dijon who became Madame Renoir in 1890.

After appearing in the 1882 Impressionist exhibition, *Luncheon* was purchased by the art dealer Paul Durand-Ruel for his family collection. The painting was infrequently seen by the public until its purchase in 1921 by the American collector Duncan Phillips, who correctly predicted that it "would bring pilgrims to pay homage from all over the civilized world." Phillips wrote of the painting: "Every inch of the canvas is alive and worth framing for itself. . . . We feel the manner of Titian and Rubens is added to the Impressionist's art of expressing the passing moment in the softness of a woman's glance, the flapping of a striped awning in a fitful breeze, the unity and vivacity of the caressing, enveloping light."

1881; Oil on canvas; 51 × 68 inches

Vincent van Gogh
Self-Portrait

THE DETROIT INSTITUTE OF ARTS

This self-portrait by Vincent van Gogh (1853–1890) is one of more than twenty he painted while living in Paris from 1886 to 1888. This period was one of the most tranquil in van Gogh's adult life; he had money, new friendships, and was experimenting enthusiastically with Impressionist color and technique. His brother Theo, with whom he shared a flat, wrote their mother: "You would not recognize Vincent, he has changed so much and it strikes other people more than it does me. He makes great progress and has begun to have some success. He is in much better spirits than before and people seem to like him. . . ."

Van Gogh came to Paris after three months' study at the Antwerp academy, where his resistance to the traditional course of study resulted in humiliating disputes. At Theo's suggestion, he took lessons with Salon painter Fernand Cormon; his fellow students included Émile Bernard and Henri de Toulouse-Lautrec. Outside the studio he met Camille Pissarro, Paul Cézanne, and Paul Gauguin and was deeply impressed by Georges Seurat's *Sunday Afternoon on the Island of La Grande Jatte* (page 80).

Van Gogh's study in Paris lightened his palette, acquainted him with the optical laws of color, and enhanced his appreciation of the linear clarity of Japanese art fashionable at the time. He often used his own features as a testing ground when experimenting with a new technique. In the Detroit painting, for example, the color dots of Seurat's *Grande Jatte* are expanded into longer strokes that clarify the facial structure and add psychological tension. In the intensity of expression some historians see a suggestion of the mental illness that would provoke the painter's suicide three years later. After meeting van Gogh in Paris, Pissarro felt that he would "either go mad or leave the Impressionists far behind. But I did not suspect," he added, "that both these presentiments would prove correct."

1887; Oil on canvas; 13¾ × 10½ inches
City of Detroit Purchase

Georges Seurat
Sunday Afternoon on the Island of La Grande Jatte
THE ART INSTITUTE OF CHICAGO

When *Sunday Afternoon on the Island of La Grande Jatte* was first shown at the Salon des Indépendants in Paris in 1886, Felix Fénéon was one of the very few critics to recognize its merits. Fénéon described the scene: "It is four o'clock on Sunday afternoon in the dog-days. On the river, swift barks dart to and fro. On the island itself a Sunday population has come together at random and from a delight in the fresh air, among the trees."

Georges Seurat (1859–1891) began making drawings of the landscape and Sunday crowds on the island of La Grande Jatte, near Asnières, in 1884. Seurat made twenty-three drawings and painted thirty-eight preparatory studies on the site; these he brought back to his studio and methodically integrated into a composition measuring approximately seven by ten feet.

The painting was finished for the 1885 exhibition at the Salon des Indépendants, but the event was canceled for lack of funds and Seurat left for Normandy to paint seascapes. There he began experimenting with small, comma-shaped brushstrokes that occasionally took the form of dots, applied over an undercoating of loosely brushed colors. These small strokes facilitated the interpenetration of light and shade and the optical interaction of complementary colors. Seurat was so impressed with this discovery that upon returning from Normandy he completely reworked *La Grande Jatte,* covering the original layer of paint with a homogeneous field of color dots.

In addition to color theory, Seurat also studied various treatises on the expressive relationships of lines and images and the logic of spatial relationships. In *La Grande Jatte* he created an atmosphere of stability and permanence by aligning figures and landscape elements with the horizontal and vertical axes of the picture frame. Line is the controlling factor, imposing coherence on the flickering interplay of pigments and introducing a formal clarity that was to be the hallmark of Neo-Impressionism.

1884–86; Oil on canvas; 81 × 120⅛ inches
Helen Birch Bartlett Memorial Collection

Henri de Toulouse-Lautrec
At the Moulin Rouge

THE ART INSTITUTE OF CHICAGO

In his early twenties Henri de Toulouse-Lautrec (1864–1901) began a lifelong association with the actresses, dancers, clowns, prostitutes, and artists of Montmartre. His greatest single source of subject matter was the dance hall and cabaret Moulin Rouge the setting of some thirty paintings. One of the most highly finished of these, *At the Moulin Rouge* documents the social diversity of the clientele. Behind a railing that separates the promenade from the dance floor sits a representative group of patrons. At the far side of the table is the music critic Edouard Dujardin, engaged in a conversation with La Macarona, one of the famous quadrille dancers. Next to her is the photographer Paul Sescau and on his left Toulouse-Lautrec's friend Maurice Guibert; the identity of the orange-haired woman is unknown. In the background arranging her hair is Louise Weber, the quadrille dancer known as La Goulue; behind her is the artist himself, his dwarfish stature accentuated by an unusually tall companion, his cousin Tapié de Céleyran. The original composition did not include the woman on the far right, identified as "Nelly C.": Lautrec added canvas to the right and bottom of the painting to introduce this garishly illuminated figure.

1892; Oil on canvas; 48½ × 55⅛ inches
Helen Birch Bartlett Memorial Collection

Henri Rousseau
The Sleeping Gypsy

THE MUSEUM OF MODERN ART · NEW YORK CITY

One of the strangest and most captivating pictures in the history of modern art, Henri Rousseau's
Sleeping Gypsy was first exhibited in Paris in the 1897 Salon des Indépendants, where a typical review
concluded, "M. Rousseau has decided to settle for the easy fame of making an utter fool of himself."

Rousseau (1844–1910), whose intentions were quite orthodox and sincere, thought of *Sleeping Gypsy*
as a genre painting and described it as follows: "A wandering Negress, playing her mandolin, with her
jar beside her (vase containing drinking water) sleeps deeply, worn out by fatigue. A lion wanders by,
detects her and doesn't devour her. There's an effect of moonlight, very poetic. . . ."

Rousseau had two primary sources of inspiration for his composition: first, a painting he very much
admired by Jean Léon Gerôme, *The Two Majesties,* which depicts a lion on a hill overlooking an arid
landscape illuminated by a full moon; second, the exotic stories about nomadic gypsies much in vogue
at the time. But most of all it was the magical powers attributed to gypsies found expression in
Rousseau's painting; the ghost of his dead wife, the artist later claimed, guided his hand during its creation.

Negative criticism delivered at the 1897 Salon apparently had no effect on Rousseau. Having acquired
considerable technical competence by 1897, the largely self-taught painter was sincerely convinced that
his work would eventually be rewarded with official glory. He thus wrote with self-confidence to the mayor
of his native city of Laval, offering to sell *Sleeping Gypsy* to the city, "for I would be happy to let the town
of Laval possess a remembrance of one of its children." His offer was not accepted.

Lost sight of for nearly two decades, the painting was rediscovered in the mid-1920s and purchased,
on the advice of Picasso, by the avant-garde American collector John Quinn. When the picture came up
for auction after Quinn's death, Surrealist poet Jean Cocteau composed a definitive summary of
Rousseau's unwitting accomplishment: "We have here the contrary of poetic painting, of anecdote. One
is confronted, rather, by painted poetry, by a poetic object."

1897; Oil on canvas; 51 × 79 inches
Gift of Mrs. Simon Guggenheim

Paul Cézanne
Still Life with Peaches and Cherries

LOS ANGELES COUNTY MUSEUM OF ART

Still Life with Peaches and Cherries dates from the 1880s, the decade in which Paul Cézanne (1839–1906) abandoned Impressionism and matured as an original artist. Cézanne last exhibited with the Impressionists in 1877; during the next few years he gradually withdrew from Paris and painted in and around his native town of Aix-en-Provence in southern France. Turning from his former interest in capturing the transient effects of light, he began his experiments with the reduction of natural form to geometric equivalents and with the perspectivic qualities of color. "I do not want to reproduce nature," he declared. "I want to recreate it."

As recreated in his still lifes, nature becomes not only a vehicle for geometric abstraction but also a medium of personal expression. In *Still Life with Peaches and Cherries,* an impossibly tipped tabletop offers an arrangement of objects seen from separate vantage points. The folds of the cloth that projects well over the table's edge form an undulating pattern corresponding to the coiled shapes of plates and fruit. Yet the work is by no means a theoretical exercise: sensitive color modulations weave all the elements into a convincing statement.

In his widely acclaimed analysis of Cézanne's still lifes, modern art historian Meyer Schapiro notes that Cézanne was particularly attracted to this genre throughout his career; one of his first works as a student was a plate of peaches, copied from a painting in the museum of Aix. Schapiro likens Cézanne's still lifes to a solitary game of pictorial chess, the artist always seeking the strongest formal position for each element of the composition. Schapiro also stresses that Cézanne was never oblivious to the beauty and poetic connotations of the objects he represented. His pieces of fruit "are often the objects of a caressing vision," says Schapiro. "He loves their asymmetrical roundness and the delicacy of their rich local color which he sometimes evokes through an exquisite rendering rarely found in his paintings of nude flesh."

Ca. 1883–87; Oil on canvas; 19¾ × 24 inches
Gift of The Adele R. Levy Fund and Mr. and Mrs. Armand S. Deutsch

America: The Nineteenth Century

Charles Willson Peale
William Smith and His Grandson

VIRGINIA MUSEUM · RICHMOND

When Baltimore merchant William Smith was elected to represent the state of Maryland in the first Congress of the United States, his son-in-law, General Otho Holland Williams, commissioned a commemorative portrait. Williams chose the most fashionable portraitist of the middle colonies, Charles Willson Peale (1741–1827), who began Smith's portrait on October 11, 1788, five days after the election. On that day Peale noted in his diary that Smith "desires me to paint his grandson in the same piece." Peale gladly obliged, creating an eccentric hybrid of state portraiture and an informal domestic scene.

Completed less than a month later, the painting represents the sitter against a backdrop of massive classical architecture symbolic of civic virtue and the ideals of the new federal government. The left third of the background, however, depicts Smith's country estate, Eutaw, named for the Battle of Eutaw Springs in which General Williams led the decisive bayonet charge. Smith's two-year-old grandson, Robert Smith Williams, holds a peach from the farm and his grandfather a peach tree branch. On the table, along with a pruning hook, is a book of John Milton's poetry and James Thompson's *Seasons*—both favorites of the artist—as well as a treatise on gardening and a copy of James Beattie's *Essay on Truth*.

An enterprising and multitalented representative of the eighteenth-century Enlightenment, Peale opened a gallery of his portraits of Revolutionary War heroes in Philadelphia in 1782; in 1786 he founded the Peale Museum of natural history. His scientific interests included the natural laws of human relationships: Marriage, he wrote, is to be conducted as a social activity designed to promote "the harmony, industry and the wealth of the nation." He saw "good government of the family" as the source of domestic contentment and enjoyed finding exemplary households among the families he was asked to paint. Thus in the Smith portrait the child, the peach, the peaceful landscape, and the grandfatherly gesture of affection also symbolize Peale's belief that familial happiness is to be cultivated like "a plant of tender growth."

1788; Oil on canvas; 51⅜ × 40¼ inches
Purchase. the Williams Fund, 1975

Thomas Cole
The Voyage of Life

MUNSON-WILLIAMS-PROCTOR INSTITUTE · UTICA, NEW YORK

By the late 1820s, Thomas Cole (1801–1848) was established as America's leading landscape painter. Emigrating from England's industrial Lancashire in 1818, Cole worked as a wood-block engraver and portrait limner in Ohio before moving to New York, where he began painting local scenery. His canvases soon found favor among New Englanders who, influenced by Wordsworth and Emerson, believed the contemplation of unspoiled nature to be morally beneficial. Revering God's visible handiwork, they preferred accurate renderings of specific scenes and cautioned artists against overuse of imagination.

Cole, however, was an incurable romantic and Platonic idealist who believed the truths of nature could never be revealed in "mere mechanical imitation." Commissions for renderings of sites in the Hudson River valley, the Catskills, and the Adirondacks, while numerous and lucrative, gradually embittered the artist against the American taste for "things, not thoughts." In 1829 Cole left for a two-year stay in Europe, where he was deeply affected by the arcadian landscapes of Claude Lorrain, the storm scenes of Salvator Rosa, and the ruins of classical antiquity. In 1832 these influences converged in *The Course of Empire,* Cole's monumental four-canvas survey of the rise and fall of Roman civilization, symbolized by changes in a single landscape at various points in history. The response to this allegorical

extravaganza was generally favorable but patrons for such large-scale cycles were hard to come by.

In 1839, Cole persuaded a wealthy New York banker, Samuel Ward, to commission a second series to be installed in the Meditation Room of his New York mansion. Plans for this four-part survey of the human condition had been outlined in Europe ten years earlier when Cole first conceived the idea of representing man as a voyager on the stream of life. In the series, Cole symbolized time and mortality with seasonal change: In *Childhood* a guardian angel launches a baby's elaborately decorated boat from a maternal cave in springtime; *Youth* himself is at the helm in the summer sun, sailing toward a celestial mirage; autumn storms threaten the bark in *Manhood;* in *Old Age* the guardian returns to direct the voyager to an opening in the winter clouds where, in Cole's words, "angels are seen descending the cloudy steps as if to welcome him to the haven of Immortal life."

After Cole's death, Ward's heirs sold *The Voyage of Life*—"something of a white elephant" in their estimation—to the American Art Union in New York. The Union gave *Voyage* its first public exhibition in 1848, offering chances to win all four paintings for a five-dollar donation. The lottery winner sold the painting to an enterprising New York religious educator who successfully marketed thousands of engraved reproductions as the "most interesting, appropriate and valuable series of family pictures in the whole world of art."

1840; Oil on canvas; each approximately 52 × 78 inches

Emanuel Leutze
Washington Crossing the Delaware

THE METROPOLITAN MUSEUM OF ART
NEW YORK CITY

In his book *A Small Boy and Others,* Henry James recalls an after-dinner outing in 1851 when he and his parents attended the first New York exhibition of Emanuel Leutze's *Washington Crossing the Delaware:* "I live again the thrill of that evening. . . . We gaped responsive to every item, lost in the marvel of wintry light, of the sharpness of the ice blocks, of the sickness of the sick soldier . . . [but] above all of the profiled national hero's purpose, as might be said, of standing *up,* as much as possible, even indeed doing it almost on one leg, in such difficulties and successfully balancing."

The German-born American painter Emanuel Leutze (1816–1868) was already a celebrity in New York before the arrival of *Washington Crossing the Delaware* from his Düsseldorf studio. His dramatic compositions documenting the evolution of religious and political freedom had been very well received and by the time he was thirty Leutze had achieved international recognition.

Continuing his series with New World freedom fighters, Leutze chose as a subject George Washington's attack on Hessian mercenaries in Trenton, New Jersey, on Christmas Day, 1776. Art gossip columns in the United States and Europe followed the painting's progress: American visitors to Düsseldorf reported being pressed into service as models; an exact copy of Washington's uniform was dispatched from the Patent Office in Washington, D.C. But when the work was in its final stages it was damaged by a fire in Leutze's studio. The second version, viewed by young Henry James, was completed in 1851.

American history students have long criticized Leutze's inaccuracies: The iron-ore boats actually used in the crossing were much larger; the officers' uniforms are inaccurate; the flag shown was not official until six months later. These observations have never reduced the painting's esteem: As the catalogue of the 1851 exhibition states, *Washington Crossing the Delaware* seems to have "power to work upon the heart."

1851; Oil on canvas; 12 feet 5 inches × 21 feet 3 inches
Gift of John Stewart Kennedy, 1897

Artist Unknown
Buffalo Hunter

Both as a romantic vision of the noble savage and an illustration of actual practice, the theme of the Indian hunting the buffalo was among the most popular in nineteenth-century American art. The buffalo was America's own mythological beast, a symbol of natural abundance doomed by manifest destiny. It came to be understood that the fate of the buffalo and that of the Indian were intertwined, a "melancholy fact" that drew artist George Catlin to the frontier in the 1830s "to snatch from hasty oblivion a truly lofty and noble race."

    The imagery of *Buffalo Hunter,* painted by an unknown primitive artist in the mid-nineteenth century, has its ultimate source in drawings by Catlin for his book on North American Indians published in 1841. These drawings were in turn adapted by Felix O. C. Darley, an illustrator who gained national recognition for his depictions of Indian life, even though he apparently never saw a real Indian or buffalo. An engraving in a magazine by Darley was the immediate source for *Buffalo Hunter.* After the painting toured Europe in the early 1950s, French writer André Malraux compared it to the work of the great naive painter Henri Rousseau (page 83). Like Rousseau's animals, the horse and buffalo seem to be magical beasts representing archetypal ideas as well as actual creatures. Both animals are simplified for theatrical effect and animated with rhythmical linear patterns that express the artist's subjective interpretation of the scene: The buffalo-monster is frightened and frightening, the white stallion instinctively alarmed but steadfast, the Indian's arrow straight and true. Clearly conveyed by this unknown painter is Catlin's description of buffalo hunts as "extraordinary (and inexpressible) exhilarations of chase, which seem to drown the prudence alike of instinct and reason."

Mid-nineteenth century; Oil on canvas; 49 × 50½ inches
Gift of Harriett Cowles Hammett Graham in memory of Buell Hammett

George Caleb Bingham
The Jolly Flatboatmen in Port

THE SAINT LOUIS ART MUSEUM

One of the first visual historians of the Western frontier was George Caleb Bingham (1811–1879). In Bingham's youth the frontier was central Missouri, where his family moved in 1819 from Virginia. There Bingham made his first paintings, rather stiff, primitively styled portraits. After study at the Pennsylvania Academy of Fine Arts he moved to Washington, D.C., and painted likenesses of prominent public figures. In his early thirties Bingham returned to Missouri and began painting local genre scenes, or, in his words, "our political and social characteristics." These pictures fall into two groups: illustrations of political campaigns—Bingham himself ran for office and served in the Missouri state legislature—and the better-known scenes of life on the Missouri and Mississippi rivers.

In the 1830s and 1840s the Missouri River was the interstate highway to the far west, where beaver pelts and buffalo hides were loaded onto flatboats and floated to markets in Saint Louis. Flatboatmen were the subjects of three paintings by Bingham; the first was completed in 1846, the last—this version —in 1857. All three canvases retain the same compositional core—a dancing boatman at the apex of a pyramid, flanked by two musicians and three onlookers in the foreground.

The central figure, whose pose is derived from a Greek statue of a dancing satyr, is linked with romantic literary visions of an American Adam living in natural paradise. Bingham's riverboatmen are never shown at work, and his paintings omit all evidence of the industry and mechanization that followed the arrival of steamboats in the 1820s. Thus what Bingham chose *not* to paint about life on the Missouri is a critical factor in interpreting his work and the American ideals it meant to convey.

1857; Oil on canvas; 47½ × 69½ inches
Purchase

Albert Bierstadt
The Sierra Nevada in California

NATIONAL MUSEUM OF AMERICAN ART
WASHINGTON, D.C.

The first major landscape painter to observe and paint West Coast mountain scenery, Albert Bierstadt (1830–1902) was responsible for establishing an idealized vision of Western landscape that persists outside the region even today. Born in Germany, Bierstadt was trained at the Düsseldorf Academy. As his work matured, he developed a technique that allowed him to create panoramas that were both very large and very detailed. This was generally accomplished by reducing or nearly eliminating the middle distance in his pictures. For example, in *The Sierra Nevada in California,* which is ten feet wide, the foreground details the flora and fauna of the region—trout, ducks, a herd of elk, native wild flowers, and small plants. Almost immediately above these small-scale forms the peaks begin to build, each increasingly more dramatic, until they are lost in turbulent clouds.

Bierstadt was at the height of his fame when *The Sierra Nevada* was first exhibited in 1868, and his work commanded the highest prices ever paid for American paintings. After viewing *The Sierra Nevada,* a London *Art Journal* critic concluded, "The most satisfactory comparison is with Nature. . . . No finer landscape has, so far as we are aware, been produced in modern times." Actually comparing *The Sierra Nevada* with nature would reveal that the cliff on the left is a modified version of a section of the north wall of Yosemite Valley and the peak at the top right resembles Mount Whitney, more than a hundred miles distant. *The Sierra Nevada* was in fact synthesized from sketches in Rome, where the artist and his wife vacationed.

Given to the National Museum of American Art in 1977 by the granddaughter of the original owner, *The Sierra Nevada* is the "most important single object ever donated to the collection" in the opinion of William Truettner, curator of eighteenth- and nineteenth-century painting and sculpture. The "dramatic means used by the artist to sum up his impressions," Truettner adds, continues to assure the painting's broad appeal.

1868; Oil on canvas; 72 × 120 inches
Bequest of Helen Huntington Hull

Frederic Edwin Church
Niagara

THE CORCORAN GALLERY OF ART · WASHINGTON, D.C.

In his instinct for showmanship, Frederic Edwin Church (1826–1900) has been described as an artistic counterpart to his contemporary, P. T. Barnum. Church's fame derived from his sensational panoramic showpieces, especially a painting of Niagara Falls as seen from the Canadian shore, near Table Rock. Exhibited to admiring crowds in New York and London, *Niagara* established Church's international reputation.

Church was the son of a wealthy Hartford insurance adjuster and was the only formal pupil of the great Hudson River landscapist Thomas Cole. After completing his studies with Cole, Church began traveling throughout the United States making landscape sketches. In 1853, he visited South America with his friend Cyrus W. Field, who later conceived and built the first transatlantic cable. During their six-month expedition, Church made geologically precise drawings of Ecuador's Cotopaxi volcano and

various sites in the Andes. He exhibited paintings based on these drawings for three years after his return, but it was not until he turned his attention to a North American landmark, Niagara Falls, that he achieved his first popular triumph.

Church's mentor Thomas Cole had considered painting the falls but instead contented himself with writing about them. "Niagara! That wonder of the world!—where the sublime and beautiful are bound together in an indissoluble chain," Cole wrote. "In its volume we conceive immensity; in its course, everlasting duration; in its impetuosity, uncontrollable power!"

In his *Niagara*, Church paid homage to Cole's sentiments by increasing the canvas width to more than twice its height, stretching the pictorial rectangle to capture the great expanse and force of the plummeting rapids. He further advanced the engulfing effect by detailing the background rather than the foreground and by placing the viewer virtually on the edge of a platform of rushing water. So precise was his suggestion of a rainbow in the upper left corner that the English critic John Ruskin refused to believe the rainbow was painted until he checked a window to assure that the glass was not the source of the prismatic effect. Other critics found in *Niagara* not only "the accuracy of a daguerreotype" but also a new rhetoric of pictorial grandeur appropriate to America's heroic destiny.

1857; Oil on canvas; 42½ × 90½ inches

Winslow Homer
Young Soldier

COOPER-HEWITT MUSEUM
THE SMITHSONIAN INSTITUTION'S
NATIONAL MUSEUM OF DESIGN
NEW YORK CITY

Winslow Homer (1836–1910) received his first formal training as an apprentice to a well-known Boston lithographer, John Bufford. Bufford owned the country's largest and most successful ` lithographic publishing company, producing a wide variety of trade cards, posters, town views, magazine illustrations, and sheet music covers, which were Homer's principal assignment during his two-year apprenticeship.

In 1857, on his twenty-first birthday, Homer left Bufford and launched himself as a free-lance illustrator. Two leading publications, *Ballou's Pictorial* and *Harper's Weekly,* soon began accepting his crisply patterned sketches of fashionable Bostonians and scenes of New England rural celebrations.

When the Civil War began, *Harper's* engaged the young free-lancer as a pictorial reporter on life in the Union Army. Homer made the first of his several visits to the front in 1861, at a time when Union forces were recovering from the loss at Bull Run. The gouache-and-oil sketch of the *Young Soldier,* which includes an unrelated pencil drawing of a soldier giving water to a wounded companion, dates from this trip; the central figure appeared as a wood engraving in the Christmas edition of *Harper's* in 1861.

Homer's Civil War sketchbooks included renderings of active combat, but most of his sketches were of life in encampments. As in *Young Soldier,* a recruit too young to fill out his bedraggled uniform, these straightforward depictions made no exceptions for the psychological wages of war. In their directness and lack of patriotic bombast, as several historians have noted, Homer's Civil War sketches prefigure the factual style of Stephen Crane's novel *The Red Badge of Courage,* published in 1893. In this book, for which *Young Soldier* could serve as an illustration, Crane stressed the anonymity of war by referring to his central character only as "the youth." "The battle was like the grinding of an immense and powerful machine to him," wrote Crane. "And the most startling thing was to learn that suddenly he was very insignificant."

1861; Oil sketch pencil and gouache on canvas; 14⅛ × 7⅛ inches
Gift of Charles Savage Homer

100

Winslow Homer
The Country School

THE SAINT LOUIS ART MUSEUM

Already established as a successful magazine illustrator, Winslow Homer (1836–1910) began painting at age twenty-five. His biographers find no record of professional painting instruction, save four or five lessons in 1861 with a New York artist named Frederic Rondel.

Homer was initially attracted to Civil War scenes but after 1865 returned to the subjects he most preferred earlier in his career—scenes of life in the country and at fashionable summer resorts. His favorite models included young children, whose outdoor activities Homer rendered with an empathetic candor reminiscent of Mark Twain.

The Country School is linked with this outdoor series because it is only nominally an indoor scene: The painting is dominated by afternoon sunlight that will ultimately reclaim the children. The anecdotal character of the composition is unambiguous and the details are charming, yet Homer's work was considered radical by some contemporary critics. "We frankly confess that we detest his subjects," wrote Henry James. "His barren plank fences, his glaring bold, blue skies . . . his freckled, straight-haired Yankee urchins, his flat-breasted maidens suggestive of a dish of rural doughnuts and pie. . . . He has chosen the least pictorial features of the least pictorial range of scenery and civilization; he has resolutely treated them as if they *were* pictorial."

James rightly observed that the artist's concerns were not limited to the achievement of picturesque effects. Homer's painting is a typical nineteenth-century genre scene but it is also a study in grouping and organization. The composition subtly plays off symmetry and asymmetry: The teacher stands at the center of the canvas but slightly to the right of the center of the blackboard; benches seem to recede equally from the corners but actually do not. This asymmetry animates the composition while the geometry of the blackboard and architecture establishes its academic ambiance. The painting's qualities thus reach beyond subject matter to the innate command of structure that repeatedly positions Homer's work among the best-regarded nineteenth-century American art.

1871; Oil on canvas; 21 × 38 inches
Purchase

Charles Christian Nahl
Sunday Morning in the Mines

CROCKER ART MUSEUM
SACRAMENTO, CALIFORNIA

Great-grandson of a renowned court sculptor for Frederick the Great, Charles Christian Nahl (1818–1878) was born in Kassel to a long-established family of German artists. He studied painting with his father at the Kassel Academy, and in 1846, moved to Paris, where he achieved recognition for his eclectically styled portraits, history paintings, and genre scenes.

Political unrest in France prompted Nahl to sail for New York in 1849. There, he heard extraordinary tales about the Gold Rush and moved to California. Nahl immediately found employment as a miner, but after prospecting for only a few months, he decided to reestablish himself as an artist. Many of his illustrations and paintings were topical or humorous, but others were of a moralizing nature, including his masterpiece *Sunday Morning in the Mines*.

A tree trunk in the center of the nine-foot painting divides the composition into two contrasting segments. On the left, aligned in a series of angles, are the wastrels: a drunken youth scattering gold dust, horse racers, brawling gamblers. On the right an arrangement of horizontal and vertical forms encloses the more virtuous group quietly observing the Sabbath: One man writes to "Dear Mother"; another reads the Bible aloud while companions launder ragged clothing in a nearby stream. Both sections are framed by botanically correct native trees and shrubs and an assortment of accurately rendered miner's tools.

The Gold Rush was already a nostalgic memory by the time *Sunday Morning in the Mines* was painted in 1872, and this nostalgia still affects California viewers. But the painting is also notable for the manner in which its organization enhances its message: Trained in the grand tradition of European history painting and at the height of his powers in the 1870s, Nahl was one of the few artists in America who could have executed such an ambitious composition.

1872; Oil on canvas; 72 × 108 inches

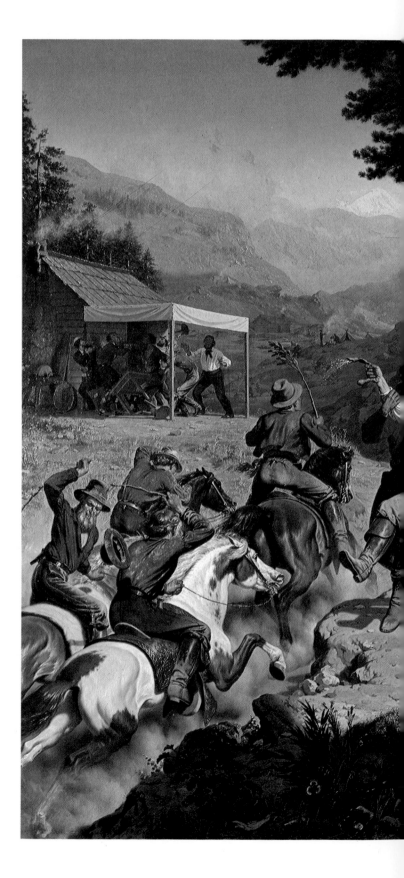

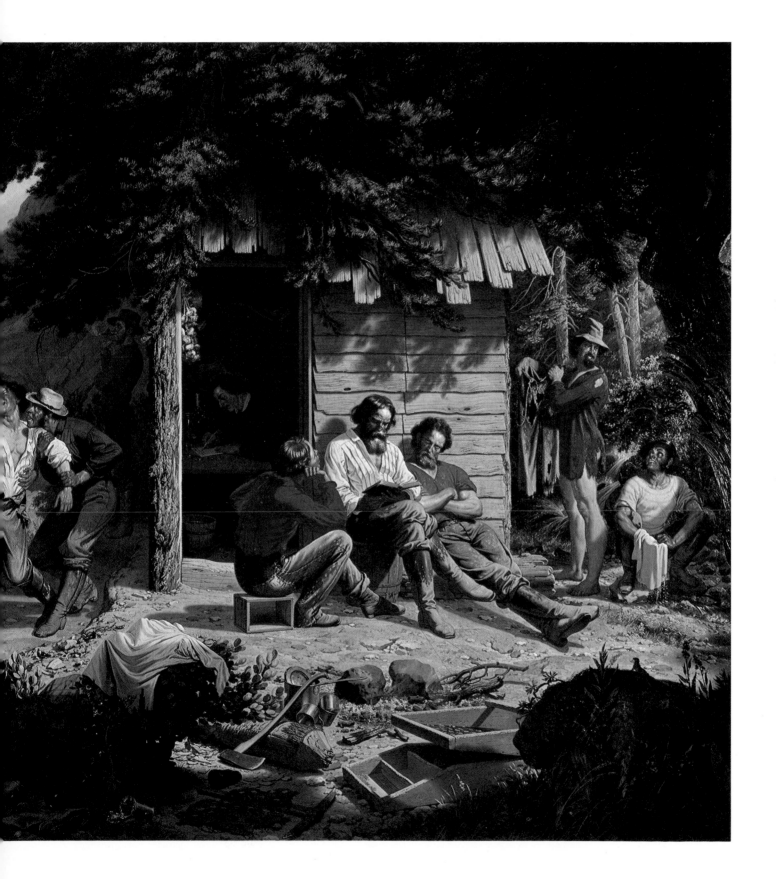

Thomas J. White (?)
Captain Jinks
of the Horse Marines

THE NEWARK MUSEUM

In the 1870s and 1880s, Samuel A. Robb's wood-carving shop on Canal Street in Manhattan offered a variety of figurative carvings for circus wagons, ship and steamboat decorations, eagles, altarpieces for Italian churches, and signs for cobblers, dentists, and druggists. The shop's specialty, however, was life-size figures for tobacconists "in great variety, on hand, and made to any design." Baseball players, squaws and Indian chiefs, and carvings of Sir Walter Raleigh wearing a sword and smoking a cigarillo were among the preferred choices. Unlike most other purveyors of wooden figures, Robb signed the carvings he completed entirely on his own, intending them to serve as demonstrations of the high quality of work available in his shop.

In 1879, Robb enlisted in the New York State National Guard and was assigned to the Twenty-second Regiment, which three years earlier provided the relief force that found the remains of Custer's Last Stand. Robb apparently made a striking impression in his double-breasted, high-collared uniform, and legend has it that another artisan employed in his shop, Thomas White (1825–1902), commemorated Robb's enlistment by carving his portrait as a tobacconist's figure, following a type known as a "dude" or "swell." The carving soon became associated with a popular Civil War–era song that satirized the pretensions of military officers, "Captain Jinks of the Horse Marines":

> I am Captain Jinks of the Horse Marines,
> I often live beyond my means,
> I sport young ladies in their teens,
> To cut a swell in the Army.

The caricature of Samuel Robb as Captain Jinks became the property of Feary's Cigar Store on Market Street in Newark, New Jersey, where it stood for nearly fifty years. The cigar business was sold in 1924 and, in appreciation of its historic relationship to the city, *Captain Jinks of the Horse Marines* was donated by a local newspaperman to the Newark Museum, where the staff finds that it continues to "arouse visions of fantasy in all."

1879; Painted wood; figure 69½ inches, base 5½ inches
Gift of Herbert E. Ehlers

Thomas Eakins
The Pathetic Song

THE CORCORAN GALLERY OF ART · WASHINGTON, D.C.

Except for one extended trip abroad, from 1866 to 1870, Thomas Eakins spent virtually all his life (1844–1916) surrounded by family and friends in Philadelphia. In Europe he studied at the École des Beaux-Arts in Paris and was deeply affected by the seventeenth-century Spanish paintings of Jusepe de Ribera and Diego Velázquez in the Prado museum. "Oh what a satisfaction it gave me to see the Spanish work so good, so strong, so reasonable, so free from every affectation," young Eakins wrote from Madrid.

Freedom from affectation and uncompromising fidelity to physical fact became the cornerstones of Eakins's own pictorial aesthetic. As an instructor and director of the Pennsylvania Academy of the Fine Arts, Eakins stressed his belief that artistic imagination and intuition must be firmly grounded in knowledge of scientific fact, particularly anatomy. Under his tenure at the academy, students were urged to draw from nude models of both sexes rather than copy casts of antique statuary. This practice, largely because it was carried out by female as well as male students, resulted in Eakins's dismissal in 1886. The incident clouded his reputation and, although highly respected by other artists, he sold few pictures during his lifetime.

Eakins' lack of commercial success was countered by the unswerving loyalty of his family and friends. Their lives and faces, uncompromisingly observed, were his principal subject matter after the late 1870s. The singer in *The Pathetic Song,* for example, is Margaret Harrison, sister of Eakins's friends Thomas Alexander and Birge Harrison, Philadelphia marine and landscape painters. The pianist is Susan Macdowell, one of Eakins's pupils, whom he married in 1884. The typical American Victorian interior, not unlike those described in Lewis Mumford's *The Brown Decades,* is rendered with a comfortable familiarity that establishes the ambiance and pleasure of a musical evening among friends. Here, as in his portraits, Eakins's realism is psychological as well as physical, capturing the moment when everyone present is absorbed by the music. The artist Fairfield Porter once wrote that Eakins "trusted his head more than his hand, and knowledge more than appearance." *The Pathetic Song* shows how much he also trusted in his friends.

1881; Oil on canvas; 45 × 32½ inches

John Singer Sargent
Fumée d'Ambre Gris

STERLING AND FRANCINE CLARK ART INSTITUTE · WILLIAMSTOWN, MASSACHUSETTS

Descended from a prominent American family that included several governors of Massachusetts, John Singer Sargent (1856–1925) was born while his parents were wintering in Florence. He was educated in Europe and traveled widely with his mother, a watercolorist, before settling in Paris to study art when he was eighteen. A precocious student, he first exhibited at the Paris Salon of 1877.

Seeking new subject matter and an exotic milieu, Sargent traveled to North Africa in 1880. There he produced a number of white-and-gray sketches of the shadowed corners and sunlit surfaces of Moorish buildings in Tangiers. *Fumée d'Ambre Gris,* which includes a young Oriental woman holding her veil over the ambergris fumes rising from an incense burner, derives from these studies.

The composition counterpoints the illuminated architecture and the white-robed woman, the naturalism of the setting heightening the figure's enigmatic pose. Henry James wrote of this picture: "I know not what this stately Mahometan may be, nor in what mysterious domestic or religious rite she may be engaged; but in her muffled contemplation and pearl-colored robes, under her plastered arcade which shines in the Eastern light, she transforms and torments us. The picture is exquisite, a radiant effect of white upon white, of similar but discriminated tones."

Completed in time for the Paris Salon of 1880, *Fumée d'Ambre Gris* made a successful appeal to the Belle Epoque taste for imaginary adaptations of oriental exotica. The figure type can be traced to studies of robed female prophets composed long before Sargent's visit to Tangiers, but the pose may derive from Sargent's observation of African culture: It has recently been suggested that the "mysterious rite" is part of a traditional Bedouin marriage ceremony in which the bride-to-be must circle an incense burner a prescribed number of times.

Although the painting's tantalizing effect resides primarily in its subject matter, its semiabstract design, the employment of light to suggest contrasts of temperature, and its many subtle gradations of white also contribute to its attraction. These technical accomplishments, allied with the provocative pose of the figure, testify to a remarkable sophistication on the part of a twenty-four-year-old painter.

1880; Oil on canvas; 54¾ × 35¹¹⁄₁₆ inches

John Singer Sargent
The Pailleron Children

DES MOINES ART CENTER

Marie-Louise and Edouard Pailleron were the children of French playwright and poet Edouard Pailleron, known for his witty studies of contemporary society and satires of academic life. Pailleron was one of Sargent's most important early patrons, commissioning a portrait of himself in early 1879. Pleased with the results, he commissioned a painting of his wife later the same year and then asked Sargent to begin a portrait of his two children. In her memoirs, *Le Paradis Perdu (Paradise Lost)*, Marie-Louise Pailleron recalls that the children's portrait by John Singer Sargent (1856–1925) required eighty-three sittings, many of which were lengthy and tempestuous. The choice of cotton or silk stockings and the arrangement of Marie-Louise's hair were among the topics of dispute, but the strong-willed character and natural restlessness of the children provoked most of the battles. When the painting was finally finished, Sargent and Marie-Louise celebrated by dancing about and throwing furnishings out the artist's mezzanine-level window. After the children departed, Sargent made a drawing of the disheveled studio and later presented it to young Mademoiselle Pailleron, inscribed "In honor of my reconciliation with terrible Marie-Louise."

Sargent's portraits are frequently criticized for submerging the personality of the sitter in self-indulgent displays of the artist's technical bravura. His double portrait of the Pailleron children, however, contradicts this assessment. It is both a brilliant painting and a striking portrait, the dramatic juxtaposition of black-and-white clothing and brushy red abstract background serving as a painterly counterpart to the intense, straightforward expressions of the children.

It was Sargent's custom to paint directly on the canvas without preliminary drawing, a practice well suited to his exuberant style of brushwork. In the children's portrait Sargent employed this technique to effect psychological tension, setting off the restrained poses of the figures against freely rendered furnishings and background. The result is a subtle suggestion of uneasiness, of fading childhood innocence, which is compounded by the knowing expression of the boy and the tense demeanor of the little girl.

Sargent's reputation waned considerably after his death in 1925, but *The Pailleron Children*, which remained in the possession of the Pailleron family in Paris until the mid-1970s, suggests that the artist possessed greater insight and a more profound command of mood than are usually credited to his work.

Ca. 1881; Oil on canvas; 60 × 69 inches
Edith M. Usry bequest in memory of her parents, Mr. and Mrs. George Franklin Usry, and additional funds donated by Dr. and Mrs. Peder T. Madsen and the Anna K. Meredith Endowment Fund

John Singer Sargent
El Jaleo

ISABELLA STEWART GARDNER MUSEUM
BOSTON, MASSACHUSETTS

After its debut at the Paris Salon of 1882, critics and public alike acclaimed *El Jaleo* the picture of the year. The largest, most imaginative, and best composed of the early works of John Singer Sargent (1856–1925), the painting was inspired by the artist's travels in Spain. Sargent's intention was to study the work of Velázquez, and he was clearly influenced by the master's silvery color harmonies and grand characterizations. He was even more captivated, however, by the half-African malagueñas and dancing performed in the cafés of Granada and Seville. Sketches of dancers, some made in Spain and others composed after Sargent's return to Paris, attempt to recreate the rhythms of the Andalusian dances and prefigure the composition of *El Jaleo*. But none combine the shadowy ambiance of a Spanish café and the theatrical lighting of a Paris nightclub so ingeniously as does the painting.

El Jaleo is the name of a Spanish song and dance that became increasingly popular after it was introduced in Jerez about 1870. In Sargent's painting, the dance serves as a point of departure for an entirely synthetic and stylized scene. The shallow space is constructed like a stage, the musicians and singers serving as backdrop to the sinuous form of the gypsy dancer. Her animated pose is heightened by the theatrical lighting, an effect Sargent reinforced by placing knobs that resembled footlights on the original frame.

Isabella Stewart Gardner, founder of the Gardner Museum, first saw and admired *El Jaleo* in the Paris Salon of 1882. But the painting was sold to T. Jefferson Coolidge of Boston. Coolidge was related to Mrs. Gardner, who persuaded him to lend the painting to her museum in 1914. That same year, she remodeled the museum's interior and built a Spanish cloister on the first floor opposite the entrance. There, in an alcove under a Moorish arch lit from below, Gardner hung *El Jaleo*. Coolidge was so delighted by the setting that he decided the painting should remain in the museum. The painting is still regarded as one of the Gardner's masterpieces, whose secret, as one critic observed, "lies entirely in the virtuosity of the execution."

1882; Oil on canvas; 94½ × 137 inches

Art of the
Twentieth Century

Pablo Picasso
Woman Ironing

THE SOLOMON R. GUGGENHEIM MUSEUM · NEW YORK CITY

At no time in Pablo Picasso's (1881–1973) long career was there a more direct relationship between his life and work than in his so-called Blue Period. The term reflects not only the artist's frequent use of blue pigments but also the subjects and mood of his pictures. During this time, from the age of twenty to twenty-three, Picasso lived in Barcelona and Madrid, finally settling in Paris. His financial condition was frequently precarious, he was lonely and in conflict about separating from his parents and adolescent milieu, and he began to feel deep compassion for the plight of the urban poor.

Woman Ironing of 1904 resembles other Blue Period paintings in its vertical isolation of a single, emaciated figure, its immobile pose, and its simplified emotional structure. Picasso's empathy for the woman's drudgery may have been augmented by his working method at the time. His friend Jaime Sabartes reported that he generally found Picasso in his studio "seated on a dilapidated chair, perhaps lower than an ordinary chair and he even seemed to prefer it as if he delighted in self-mortification and enjoyed subjecting his spirit to tortures so long as they spur him on. The canvas was placed on the lowest part of the easel and this compelled him to paint in an almost kneeling position."

The elongation and angular deformation of Picasso's Blue Period figures are often attributed to the influence of El Greco and to medieval Catalan sculpture he knew as a youth. These models encouraged Picasso to subordinate naturalism to personal expression, enabling him to create forms that seem to live even more intensely than real-life counterparts.

1904; Oil on canvas; 45¾ × 28⅛ inches
The Justin K. Thannhauser Collection

Vasily Kandinsky
Black Lines

THE SOLOMON R. GUGGENHEIM MUSEUM · NEW YORK CITY

As an adolescent Vasily Kandinsky (1866–1944) became convinced that each color had a mystical life of its own, including a correspondence with musical sound. These unusual feelings about color persisted as he obtained a degree in law and economics at the University of Moscow. In 1896 Kandinsky was offered a professorship in jurisprudence but, succumbing to what he called a "now or never" mood, he refused the offer and took a train to Munich to study painting. He obtained a diploma from the Munich Academy in 1900 and during the next few years enjoyed moderate success with a variety of painting styles influenced by avant-garde French art.

In 1909 Kandinsky settled into a house in the small Bavarian town of Murnau, where he made a historic leap into purely abstract art. Much impressed at the time with the utopian doctrines of theosophy, Kandinsky felt that the spiritual deficiencies of mankind were due to its obsessive attachment to the material universe. New forms of art must be developed, he concluded, to prepare man for the future world where all forms of materialism would be transcended. He began systematically moving his work away from representations of physical objects, seeking instead a method of depicting the inner realm of the spirit. Kandinsky's first completely abstract works were based on landscape motifs and date from about 1910. By 1913 he had advanced to lyric compositions such as *Black Lines,* one of the few oils of that year, according to Kandinsky, that did not derive from any physical source. Kandinsky scholar Rose-Carol Long suggests that the flowerlike patches of color might be a visual fulfillment of theosophist Rudolf Steiner's description of "spiritland," where amorphous colors float and intermingle. The lush colors are related to those Kandinsky employed in earlier works devoted to the theme of the Garden of Love; in *Black Lines* the garden floats in cosmic space where, in Kandinsky's view, visual harmonies echo "the symphony we call the music of the spheres."

1913; Oil on canvas; 51¼ × 51⅜ inches
The Solomon R. Guggenheim Collection

Tom Thompson
The Jack Pine

One of Canada's most venerated national icons, *The Jack Pine* marks the culmination of Tom Thompson's (1877–1917) brief and remarkable artistic career. Thompson grew up in Ontario near Owen Sound on Georgian Bay. He became a machinist's apprentice, attended business college, and worked as a photoengraver in Seattle before settling in Toronto in 1905. For the next several years he was employed by several Toronto graphic art firms, where his colleagues included early Canadian modern artists Fred Varley and J. E. H. MacDonald.

Thompson was a sporadic, self-taught hobby painter and made several oil sketches during a vacation trip to Algonquin Park in northern Ontario in 1912. Impressed by the sketches, Thompson's friends and colleagues urged him to try a full-scale canvas. The result was *Northern Lake,* a richly toned, broadly painted view of a lake framed by bare trees. Thompson submitted the canvas to the 1913 Ontario Society of Artists' annual exhibition where, much to his surprise, the painting was purchased by the government of Ontario.

Restless and unsettled, Thompson spent the next two years summering in the woods and wintering in Toronto. In the spring of 1916 he visited the remote Little Cauchon Lake at the northern end of Algonquin Park and sketched a view of the lake through the branches of a solitary pine tree. Back in Toronto in the winter of 1916–17, he transformed the sketch into *The Jack Pine* painting.

Contrasting bold, slashing brushwork with delicate, tracerylike drawing, Thompson's radiant composition suggests the stillness that presages a thunderstorm. Critics saw the solitary pine as an emblem of the north, and the entire composition as a poetic meditation upon the strength and primitive beauty of the Canadian wilderness. In 1918 the canvas was purchased by the National Gallery of Canada, which later authorized thousands of reproductions for public buildings and a *Jack Pine* postage stamp. The artist, unfortunately, knew nothing of this success: In 1917 he left the canvas in his Toronto studio and departed for his annual trip to Algonquin Park where, four months later, he drowned in Canoe Lake.

1916–17; Oil on canvas; 50¼ × 55 inches

Paul Klee
Red Balloon

THE SOLOMON R. GUGGENHEIM MUSEUM · NEW YORK CITY

For Paul Klee (1879–1940) artistic creation was a profound kind of play. "Just as a child imitates us in his playing," Klee said, "we in our playing imitate the forces which created and create the universe." Art making is thus an instrumental process, forging new realities that extend beyond the visible into the realm of psychic experience. Traditional art forms resulted in "excellent pictures of the surfaces of things," in Klee's estimation, but they neglected "nonoptical impressions and images." Klee's special gifts included a capacity for giving his "nonoptical impressions" a visible form that appears childishly simple, yet eludes literal interpretation.

Red Balloon was painted in 1922, two years after Klee joined the staff of the Bauhaus School in Weimar. There his position as instructor of painting compelled him to formulate a concrete pedagogical system to communicate previously intuitive observations. A work of art is "constructed piece by piece," he concluded, "exactly like a house." *Red Balloon* demonstrates one of Klee's formulas for building a rhythmic composition. Rhythm can be accomplished, Klee told his students, by opposing a structured plane—in this case the left side of the painting—with an unstructured plane—here the right side—"in such a way that the two types of planes alternate both horizontally and vertically."

One of the least likely conclusions to be drawn about *Red Balloon,* however, is that it is essentially a pedagogical exercise. The painting's joyful colors still echo the revelation Klee experienced while painting in Tunisia in 1914. There Klee suddenly felt "possessed by color—I do not need to pursue it. I know that it will possess me forever. This is the great moment; color and I are one."

As for the specific iconography of his pictures, Klee had little to say. The motif of the balloon occurs periodically in paintings and watercolors of the 1920s: here its presence reminds us of Klee's conviction that art, like the balloon, can offer us the possibility of "a change of point of view just as we have a change of air."

1922; Oil on chalk-primed gauze; 12½ × 12¼ inches
The Solomon R. Guggenheim Collection

George Bellows
Dempsey and Firpo

WHITNEY MUSEUM OF AMERICAN ART
NEW YORK CITY

By his mid-twenties, George Bellows (1882–1925) was already known as *the* American artist. His large and virile industrial landscapes, New York street scenes, and illustrations of athletic combat were publicly embraced as embodiments of the health and virtues of American democracy. Bellows was in fact a philosophical anarchist and a regular contributor to the radical publication *The Masses*. But like his similarly inclined colleague John Sloan, Bellows rarely permitted his political sentiments to surface in his painting, preferring instead to elaborate the picturesque vitality of ordinary American life.

Among Bellows's best-known works are paintings of boxers. Bellows himself was an athlete: while studying painting with Robert Henri, he played semiprofessional baseball on weekends. Sharkey's athletic club, near Henri's studio on upper Broadway in New York, was the setting for his freely brushed pre-1910 boxing scenes. After 1918 Bellows's style was radically altered by his conversion to a geometrical composition system termed dynamic symmetry. This system, together with his work in lithography, increased Bellows's emphasis on pictorial structure and restrained his dynamic brushwork. Thus while the 1924 *Dempsey and Firpo* resembles its predecessors in its freezing of a dramatic moment, it differs radically in surface treatment.

Dempsey and Firpo resulted from Bellows's assignment by the New York *Evening Journal* as a visual reporter for a fight pairing heavyweight champion Jack Dempsey, the "Manassa Mauler," with Argentine challenger Luis Firpo, the "Wild Bull of the Pampas." During the first round Dempsey floored Firpo seven times but Firpo also knocked Dempsey out of the ring into the first row of spectators. Bellows, who included his self-portrait in the far left-hand corner of the composition, captured Dempsey's ignominious exit from the ring. Bellows also made a lithograph of the same composition whose brisk sales resulted in *Dempsey and Firpo*'s widespread acclaim.

1924; Oil on canvas; 51 × 63 inches

Arshile Gorky
The Artist and His Mother

WHITNEY MUSEUM OF AMERICAN ART · NEW YORK CITY

A seminal figure in the development of American Abstract Expressionism, Arshile Gorky (1904–1948) was born Vosdanik Manoog Adoian in Khorkom, a small village in Turkish Armenia. In 1908 his father immigrated to the United States to avoid conscription into the Turkish army, leaving behind a wife and four children. Gorky's mother, Lady Shushanik, was descended from a noble family whose lineage extended to the fifth century and included architects, artists, and Apostolic priests. She decided her son should devote his life to aesthetic beauty, although his specific vocation remained uncertain. Political turmoil disrupted the boy's formal education: In Gorky's youth Armenia underwent Turkish genocide, civil war, World War I, and the Bolshevik Revolution. In 1916 his older brother and sister left for America; Gorky, his mother, and his younger sister, Vartoosh, were left behind. The family became impoverished and Lady Shushanik fell ill from malnutrition. After being refused admission to a charity hospital because she had a husband in the United States, Gorky's thirty-nine-year-old mother died of starvation in March 1919.

In 1920 Gorky and Vartoosh immigrated to America. He changed his name to Arshile—a variant of Achilles—Gorky—a tribute to the Russian writer Maxim Gorky. After a series of odd jobs he enrolled at the Rhode Island School of Design. In his early work he emulated the great modern masters, particularly Cézanne, Kandinsky, Miró, and, above all, Picasso. Later he turned to Surrealism, which provided a means for developing his own spontaneous abstract style.

Gorky probably began working on the double portrait of himself and his mother in 1926. The motif was provided by a photograph of the two taken in 1912 to send to his father in America, and the painting marks the beginning of Gorky's reliance on his own psyche as a source of artistic inspiration. With cool colors he underscored the dignity and solemnity of his mother's face and infused the scene with a mood of dreamy melancholy. Gorky's sister Vartoosh said of the painter: "Mother made Gorky an artist. . . . 'Someday,' he told me, 'my paintings of Mother will make her live forever.' And he never forgot, even in America. He painted her, he drew her with all of his soul."

1926–29; Oil on canvas; 60 × 50 inches
Gift of Julien Levy for Maro and Natasha Gorky in memory of their father

Emily Carr
Forest, British Columbia

VANCOUVER ART GALLERY

"Sketching in the woods is wonderful," wrote Emily Carr (1871–1945). "You spread your camp stool and look around. 'Don't see much here. Wait. . . .' Slowly things begin to move, to slip into their places. Groups and masses and lines tie themselves together. Colors you had not noticed come out timidly or boldly. In and out, in and out your eye passes. . . . Here is a picture, a complete thought; and there another and another."

Canada's first major woman modern artist, Carr grew up in Victoria, British Columbia. She studied at the California School of Design in San Francisco and in 1899 enrolled in London's Westminster School of Art. In 1910 she traveled to Paris, where she exhibited in the 1911 Salon d'Automne along with Fernand Léger, Juan Gris, and Robert Delaunay. Returning to Victoria in 1912, she found it necessary to open a boardinghouse to support herself and had little time for painting.

The turning point in Carr's life came in 1927 when she was fifty-six years old. Invited to participate in a major exhibition of modern art mounted by the National Gallery of Canada, Carr became acquainted with Lawren Harris and other leading Canadian modern artists. The experience was a revelation that sent Carr back to her easel, where she began creating the Canadian visual mythology that was her greatest achievement.

Carr perceived the wilderness as did the Northwest Coast Indians—a brooding presence, beautiful but forbidding. Her forests are repositories of life force where light assumes its primal role of fostering growth. "People curse this great force," lamented Carr, "curse it for a useless litter because it yields no income. Run fire through this green sea, break it, make it black and frightful, tear out its roots. Leave it unguarded, forsaken and from the bowels of the earth rushes again the great green ocean of growth."

With such paintings as *Forest, British Columbia,* Carr evolved a personal style that was both a vehicle for her own emotions and an objective observation of natural forces. This gives Carr's work its unique tension, says Carr biographer Doris Shadbolt, "so that to know her paintings is to know both Emily Carr and the forest, and each with a sense of heightened awareness."

1931–32; Oil on canvas; 51 × 34 inches

Edward Hopper
Nighthawks

THE ART INSTITUTE OF CHICAGO

A particular favorite of the artist, Edward Hopper's (1882–1967) *Nighthawks* was "suggested by a restaurant on Greenwich Avenue [New York] where two streets meet. *Nighthawks* seems to be the way I think of a night street. . . . I simplified the scene a great deal and made the restaurant bigger. Unconsciously, probably, I was painting the loneliness of a large city."

Nighthawks is also a study of light flooding through a window, a dominant motif in Hopper's work. The glass insulates the inside world from the outside, observer from observed, subject from object, and yet, in a tentative way, suggests their union. The window is the source of theatrically focused light that links the restaurant and the empty street, creating, as Hopper said, "the sensation for which so few try, of the interior and exterior of a building seen simultaneously."

Hopper's devotion to commonplace urban scenes can be traced to his study with Robert Henri, who championed the genre in the early 1900s. Hopper acknowledged his debt to Henri but concluded that his master overemphasized subject matter at the expense of form and design. "It took me ten years to get over Henri," Hopper said later. Between 1906 and 1910 Hopper traveled three times to Europe, where he admired Courbet and the Impressionists but did not deviate from his basically realistic style. He supported himself as a commercial illustrator until 1924, when financial circumstances permitted full-time work as a painter.

After the mid-1920s and throughout Hopper's long career his work remained surprisingly consistent, forming a long series of meditations on the transitory aspects of American life, illuminated architecture, and urban estrangement. Hopper said that he painted what he saw, and in his eyes familiar scenes were infused with mystery. As former Whitney Museum director Lloyd Goodrich, a friend of the artist for more than forty years, concisely stated, "For all his realism, Hopper was essentially a poet."

1942; Oil on canvas; 30 × 60 inches
Friends of American Art Collection

Diego Rivera
The Flower Carrier

SAN FRANCISCO MUSEUM OF MODERN ART

Many local visitors to the San Francisco Museum of Modern Art, the museum reports, regard Diego Rivera (1886–1957) as one of "their" artists. Rivera worked in San Francisco in the first and last years of the 1930s and his visits made a profound impression on the city's artists and intelligentsia.

In the United States, Rivera was the best known of the Mexican artists who precipitated the great revival of mural painting in the 1920s. His simple, stylized depictions of the plight and heroism of the Indian, peon, and peasant mother were intended above all to serve the aims and aspirations of worldwide communist revolution. When Rivera was invited to San Francisco to paint murals commemorating California's financial progress for the new $2.5 million Stock Exchange Building in 1930, the irony was not lost on local artists. Painter Maynard Dixson told the press, "I believe he is the greatest living artist . . . [but] the Stock Exchange could look the world over without finding a man more inappropriate for the part than Rivera."

Complaints ceased when Rivera and his wife, Frida Kahlo, arrived in the city, where the exotic couple was feted with endless teas, dinners, and weekends. Rivera lectured frequently about his political and aesthetic theories and inspired a number of local artists to investigate fresco painting. His name and work rarely left the front pages as he completed the Stock Exchange mural and another for the San Francisco Art Institute. Upon his departure in 1931 the San Francisco *News* editorialized: "California's native painters will all profit by the exploitation of Rivera in recent months; it has meant an enormous stimulation of public interest in art."

One of Rivera's San Francisco patrons, bibliophile Albert Bender, decided to assure this interest by donating a number of works by Rivera to the San Francisco Museum of Modern Art. Among these was *The Flower Carrier*, sometimes called *The Flower Vendor*. A panel painting, *The Flower Carrier* dates from 1935, the year Rivera stopped receiving mural commissions from the Mexican government, which had by then come to regard his work as insufficiently realistic.

1935; Oil and tempera on panel; 47¾ × 47¾ inches
Gift of Albert M. Bender, memorial to Caroline Walter

Henri Matisse
The Thousand and One Nights

MUSEUM OF ART, CARNEGIE INSTITUTE · PITTSBURGH, PENNSYLVANIA

During the last years of his life, Henri Matisse (1869–1954) devoted most of his creative energies to the systematic exploration of a new technique, the paper cutout. Although he had used cutouts as compositional aids in the 1930s, Matisse began concentrating on the medium in its own right while bedridden after a serious operation in 1941. To create a cutout, he first selected several large sheets of paper previously painted with opaque watercolor by assistants. From these brightly colored sheets, Matisse cut out with a scissors patterns and organic shapes analogous to those he used in his paintings —serpentines, palm fronds, leaves, stripes, and flowers. The cutout forms were then pinned to furniture or walls near his bed and then were shifted about and combined into various compositions.

Films of Matisse at work in the 1940s document his technique: He held the scissor blades wide open except when forming a sharp curve or angle. His hand moved in rapid, graceful swoops across the

paper, which the scissors touched only at the point where the cutting edges of the blades meet. "Cutting straight into color," Matisse remarked, "reminds me of the direct carving of the sculptor . . . one movement linking line with color, contour with surface."

While the cutout forms emerged quickly and spontaneously, the opposite was true of their placement and organization. The components of *The Thousand and One Nights,* for example, were fixed at random on Matisse's wall for several months before he brought them together in a composition based on Sergei Diaghilev's 1910 ballet *Schéhérazade.* The patterns and shapes allude to recurrent themes in the tales of the Arabian Nights: the magical lamp, first shown at night and then silhouetted against the dawn, wisps of smoke, a storm at sea, and a cave. The text in cutout lettering translates "She saw the light of day/she fell discreetly silent," referring to the moment when the stories ended and the magic ceased. The fruit and plant forms suggest the sensuous imagery of the tales while the heart shapes signal the overriding theme of love. Late works such as *The Thousand and One Nights* mark the culmination of Matisse's lifelong preoccupation with abstract symbolic form and are justly celebrated as one of the triumphant late flowerings in the history of modern art.

1950; Gouache on cut and pasted paper; 54¾ × 147¼ inches
Museum Purchase: Acquired through the generosity of the Sarah Mellon Scaife family, 1971

Jackson Pollock
Autumn Rhythm

THE METROPOLITAN MUSEUM OF ART · NEW YORK CITY

"My painting," wrote Jackson Pollock (1912–1956), "does not come from the easel. I prefer to tack the unstretched canvas to the hard wall or the floor. . . . On the floor I am more at ease. I feel nearer, more a part of the painting, since this way I can walk around it, work from four sides, and literally be *in* the painting. . . . When I am *in* my painting, I'm not aware of what I'm doing. It is only after a sort of 'get acquainted' period that I see what I've been about. I have no fears about making changes, destroying the image etc., because the painting has a life of its own. I try to let it come through. It is only when I lose contact with the painting that the result is a mess. Otherwise there is pure harmony, an easy give and take, and the painting comes out well."

One of the most innovative and influential twentieth-century American artists, Pollock studied under Midwestern realist painter Thomas Hart Benton at the Art Students League in New York. After working for the WPA's Federal Art Project from 1938 to 1942, Pollock began developing his own highly personal abstract style. Picasso's Expressionistic canvases of the 1930s and Surrealist techniques for liberating subconscious thought provided springboards for Pollock's own spontaneous working methods, including his famous technique of dripping or splattering industrial pigments on the canvas with long sticks instead of brushes. Pollock's employment of this technique reached a climax in 1950 in huge paintings such as *Autumn Rhythm,* where dancelike movements of the artist's entire body are recorded with ecstatic whips of paint. The uncharacteristically natural colors of *Autumn Rhythm,* painted in September or October of 1950, evoke the idea of landscape, prompting frequent comparisons between Pollock's work and Claude Monet's laterally expanded water lily paintings (page 62).

1950; Oil and enamel on canvas; 8 feet 10½ inches × 17 feet 8 inches
George A. Hearn Fund, 1957

Jasper Johns
Three Flags

WHITNEY MUSEUM OF AMERICAN ART
NEW YORK CITY

When he was twenty-four, Jasper Johns (1930–) dreamed he was painting an American flag. Soon after, he made a number of flag paintings whose banality, realism, impersonality, and flatness contradicted nearly all the major tenets of the reigning Abstract Expressionist style. Rather than pictures of flags, Johns made replicas, filling his canvas from edge to edge to achieve total identity of subject matter and picture surface. Because they were painted in encaustic, a technique which mixes pigments with hot wax that retains the track of the brush, Johns's flags could not be confused with real flags; yet the identity of image and surface made critics uncomfortable about calling them "representations" of flags. Johns's flag canvases thus pose a question about the difference between art and reality or, more specifically, about the concepts used to distinguish one from the other.

Three Flags, painted in 1958, is constructed from three progressively smaller American flag canvases attached one atop another. The idea "came to me all at once," Johns said, "the thought was complete. . . . I was eager to start the picture; I remember I had to wait for the canvas stretchers to be made specially; they had to be bolted to one another. And I remember having a kind of moral conflict about whether to paint the covered portions, because the idea of doing work which will be covered, and therefore not a part of the necessary information about the picture—that idea conflicts with the teasing quality of the picture which suggests that you should have done it." In the end, Johns painted the covered areas gray.

The teasing quality of *Three Flags* also extends to its spatial construction: It is literally a three-dimensional picture of two-dimensional forms. In one sense it is a single painting; in another, three paintings. Johns himself relates the composition to the familiar illustration of the girl on the Morton's salt box who carries a salt box with the same illustration which in turn repeats the image. Through its paradoxical structure, *Three Flats* forces the spectators into an intense confrontation with the image so that, in Johns's words, they must "look at an object that is really never seen."

1958; Encaustic on canvas; 30⅞ × 45½ inches
50th Anniversary Gift of the Gilman Foundation, Inc., The Lauder Foundation, A. Alfred Taubman, an anonymous donor (and purchase)

Lucas Samaras
Mirrored Room

ALBRIGHT-KNOX ART GALLERY · BUFFALO, NEW YORK

"If a visitor were to see one work only," according to the Albright-Knox Art Gallery, "the *Mirrored Room* would be the certain choice." Acquired in 1966, Lucas Samaras's (1936–   ) *Mirrored Room* measures eight feet in width, ten feet in depth, and eight feet in height. Inside and out, the cubicle is covered with 24-inch-square mirrors. The single source of light is the open door, and the interior contains a table and chair, also made entirely of mirrors.

Critic Robert Hughes describes *Mirrored Room*'s effect upon the viewer: "To enter . . . is to see oneself reflected to infinity, fragment by fragment, never whole but indefinitely expanding in detail; to be multiplied thus, with every gesture held by the glass in dwindling, staccato multiplication beyond the limit of sight, is a strange feat of narcissism. At the same time the mirrors compose something very much larger than the self, an illusion of twinkling infinity where all solid location is lost, like the night sky or outer space."

A Greek immigrant, Samaras came to the United States in 1948 and studied at Rutgers University and in Columbia University's graduate program in art history. He was attracted to artists working in unorthodox media and around 1960 began experimenting with fantastic or fetishistic assembled objects, often enclosed in boxes. Later he began altering the interiors of the boxes, sometimes with mirrors, to suggest hidden chambers.

The boxes were modestly sized until 1964, when Samaras recreated his own bedroom in a boxlike full-scale environment called *Room No. 1. Room No. 2,* later retitled *Mirrored Room,* came about because "since the bedroom was a real, autobiographical room, I was searching for an idea to create some other kind of room, an abstract, geometric or theoretical room. As it developed, the *Mirrored Room* was such a thing. I included a table and chair . . . for someone to sit down and imagine or think or discover. . . . [People] paint with their bodies when they enter the room; you know, they inspect themselves, 'paint' themselves; they scribble. Then they go away and the scribble goes away too—kind of an instant erasure."

1966; Mirrors on a wooden frame; 8 × 8 × 10 feet
Gift of Seymour H. Knox, 1966

Larry Bell
Untitled

THE OAKLAND MUSEUM · OAKLAND, CALIFORNIA

Perhaps the most seductive of the new, semitechnological art associated with Los Angeles in the mid-1960s are the mirrored glass cubes of Larry Bell (1939–   ). Bell started as a painter of shaped canvases, but by 1963 he was working with shape directly in a series of small mirrored boxes faced with ellipses or linear patterns. In 1964 he began using squares of glass chemically coated in a vacuum chamber to bend light waves, resulting in reflective surfaces with very subtle rainbow tints. Like those in an oil slick, these colors have no pigments and are created by the interaction of various spectral wavelengths with the human eye.

Dissatisfied with the coatings applied commercially, Bell had a special vacuum chamber built for his studio and learned the complex technical process himself. Soon he was working with larger surfaces, such as the three-foot-square panels of the cube in the Oakland Museum. With this change of scale, Bell's forms attained true—if paradoxically immaterial—sculptural presence.

Bell's cubic sculptures are chimerical arenas of transparency and reflection. Environmental elements seen through and reflected by the glass merge optically with the enclosed space of the cube; for the viewer, these effects can be profoundly disorienting. His surfaces dissolve the boundary between solid objects and empty space, between what is actually visible through the transparent sections of the glass and what is reflected from without. Bell's objective was, in part, to demonstrate that an apparently empty enclosure can be full of light, movement, and color, a revelation intended to promote a self-conscious awareness of the mechanics of visual perception.

1967; Coated glass; 36¼ × 36¼ × 36¼ inches
The Carl A. Rietz Collection, courtesy of the Concours d'Antiques, Oakland Museum Association

Robert Indiana
Love

INDIANAPOLIS MUSEUM OF ART

Opposite the title page of their book *Icons and Images of the Sixties,* critics Nicolas and Elena Calas printed a photograph of Robert Indiana (1928–   ) atop his twelve-foot sculpture *Love.* It would be difficult to name a more appropriate illustration. As a poster and in the form of the largest commemorative stamp issue ever authorized by the U.S. Post Office, Indiana's four-letter design became an unofficial logo of '60s counterculture.

Visually, the bold pattern of stenciled letters align *Love* squarely with '60s Pop Art. Asked to define Pop, Indiana replied, "Pop *is* love, in that it accepts all . . . all the meaner aspects of life which, for various aesthetic and moral considerations, other schools of painting have rejected or ignored. Pop is still pro-art, but surely not art for art's sake. [Pop's] participants are not intellectual, social or artistic malcontents with furrowed brows and fur-lined skulls."

Indiana's principal contribution to the Pop Art repertory was the road sign, the forms and vocabularies of which he reorganized into colorful geometric designs. All the signs in Indiana's work are said to relate to personal experience. The design for *Love,* for example, is descended from a painting titled *Love Is God,* which reversed a "God Is Love" sign posted in a Christian Science church Indiana attended with his mother. He later extracted the single word "love" and isolated it within a new design, where it can still be interpreted as a moral injunction.

"The word and its symbolic implication and the fact that it is the creation of perhaps the most important living artist in the state of Indiana," says Indianapolis Museum of Art Director Robert Yassin, have helped make the *Love* image "a symbol for the museum and also for the city of Indianapolis."

1966; Acrylic on canvas; 71⅞ × 71⅞ inches
James E. Roberts Fund

Richard Estes
Helene's Florist

Of all Photo-Realist painters, Richard Estes (1936–   ) is perhaps the most highly regarded. Trained at The Art Institute of Chicago, he worked as an advertising illustrator and layout designer in New York from 1959 until 1966, when he became a full-time painter. His compositions are based on 35mm color photographs of New York street scenes he shoots and develops himself. Unlike many Photo-Realist painters who transfer images directly from projected slides to canvases, Estes uses photographs as preliminary sketches, synthesizing information from several shots of the same scene. "I use photographs because I find it gives me the best references in the subject I choose to paint," Estes says, "[but] I don't believe the photograph is the last word in realism. . . . I can select what to do or what not to do from what's in the photograph. I can add or subtract from it. . . . So what I'm trying to paint is not something different but something more like the place I've photographed. Somehow the paint and the intensity of the color emphasize the light and do things to build up form that a photograph does not do. In that way the painting is superior to the photograph."

Helene's Florist is a frontal view of a flower shop and neighboring businesses on Columbus Avenue at 72nd Street in Manhattan. Underpainted in acrylic and overpainted in oil, the picture is flawlessly crafted to the last detail, including the artist's signature inserted in the menu listings of the diner. Unlike a typical snapshot, Estes's composition provides a razor-sharp double perspective that combines both interior and exterior views. The painting also deviates from its photographic counterpart in its careful tonal control and total absence of urban grime. *Helene's Florist* is thus far from a mechanical reproduction: "If I have to choose between authenticity and making a good painting," Estes admits, "I'd rather have a good painting."

1971; Oil on canvas; 48 × 72 inches
Gift of Edward Drummond Libbey

Richard Estes
Supreme Hardware Store

THE HIGH MUSEUM OF ART
ATLANTA, GEORGIA

Richard Estes (1936–   ) began painting long vistas of New York City streets in 1972. These compositions, such as *Supreme Hardware Store,* multiply the opportunities for capturing reflections in glass, one of Estes's signature effects. In *Supreme Hardware Store* each window is a cityscape in itself. The glass, besides permitting access to shop interiors, also expands the composition to include the other side of the street.

In counterpoint to the animated complexity of the window surfaces is the complete absence of actual human activity. Estes stopped including figures in his paintings in 1970 because "the backgrounds just seemed more fascinating than the figures." More fundamentally, Estes concluded that if a figure appeared in his painting "it becomes romanticized—a period piece like Edward Hopper. It changes one's reaction to the painting . . . because when you add figures then people start relating to the figures and it's an emotional relationship. The painting becomes too literal, whereas without the figure it's more purely a visual experience."

Estes's emphasis on the visual rather than emotional aspects of aesthetic experience relates his work to the mainstream of American contemporary art. Like many of the major artists of the 1970s, Estes is firm in his conviction that art "isn't done with one's emotions; it's done with the head."

1973; Oil on canvas; 40 × 66¼ inches
Gift of Virginia Carroll Crawford

Paul Manship
Briseis

MINNESOTA MUSEUM OF ART · SAINT PAUL

Most often remembered today for his Prometheus
Fountain in New York's Rockefeller Center, Paul
Manship (1885–1966) was at the top of his
profession in the 1930s. Born and raised in Saint
Paul, Manship dropped out of high school to
devote himself to art. Discovering that he was
color-blind, he resolved to become a sculptor. He
studied at New York's Art Students League and at
the studio of Solon and Gutzon Borglum, the latter
the sculptor of Mount Rushmore. From 1909 to
1912 he was at the American Academy in Rome,
where he was deeply impressed by classical art,
particularly archaic Greek sculpture. This influence
is clearly evident in his mature work, which
typically combines stylized renditions of archaic
Greek heads with elongated, naturalistic bodies.

Briseis, first exhibited in 1916, drew special praise
from the writer Booth Tarkington, who compared
it to a musical composition by Johannes Brahms.
The figure's somewhat wistful expression and
sensual anatomy are appropriate to the story of
Briseis in the *Iliad.* After killing her husband,
parents, and three brothers in a sack of their city,
Achilles carried away Briseis as his slave. She was
soon much loved by her master, who was forced to
give her up to King Agamemnon. Achilles sulked in
his tent, refusing to fight, and the Greeks lost
ground daily. Patroclus, Achilles's dearest friend,
went to the field in his stead and was slain. Achilles
returned to action, avenged the death of Patrocles
by slaying Trojan Prince Hector, and was reunited
with Briseis.

Manship remained steadfast to the stylistic
conventions of Greek art throughout his long
career, maintaining that these forms represented an
ageless standard of excellence. His work is original,
nevertheless, and reflective of his own time: To
create it, Manship said, was always a "true joy."

1950, after an original of 1916; Marble; 27 inches high; base 3 × 7¼ × 6
inches
Photograph: Jerry Mathiason

Betye Saar
Indigo Mercy

THE STUDIO MUSEUM IN HARLEM
NEW YORK CITY

As a young child Betye Saar (1926–   ) remembers being clairvoyant: "I could see things. Some afternoons I would say, 'Oh-oh. Daddy's really mad. He missed his bus.' And then the telephone would ring and it would be he saying, 'I'm really mad. I missed my bus.' That was unsettling for my family."

Saar lost her clairvoyance at age six when her father died. But she remained attracted to the occult and studied the symbols and ritual ceremonies of various supernatural systems. Like the shells and stones she hoarded as a young girl, this inquiry provided a number of small but intriguing revelations that would ultimately coalesce into a personal art form.

Saar was raised in Los Angeles where she watched Simon Rodia assemble his fantastic Watts Towers. After graduation from the University of California as a design major in 1949, she became a graphic designer and then turned to etching and printmaking. In the late 1960s a Pasadena exhibition of Joseph Cornell boxes containing astrological signs stimulated Saar to experiment with her own mixed-media compositions. The box format proved to be especially compatible with her passion for collecting small objects relating to her family and the occult, and these materials soon found their way into her assemblages. Many of these compositions are feminine and personal; others have a very broad autobiographical dimension in their references to black liberation movements and sexual stereotyping of black women.

In 1973 Saar began creating freestanding boxes that resembled altars, often featuring drawers or windows that contain fetishistic and voodoolike objects. *Indigo Mercy,* which calls to mind a vanity table or a family heirloom, incorporates pins, keys, beads, mirrors, feathers, candles, and a ceremonial doll—objects intended to impart energies from their previous existences. This dressing table–altar is at the same time an intimate collage and a ritual form suggesting communal beliefs. Most of all it is an individualistic feminine statement—as Saar says of herself, "I never had the stroke for 'mainstream,' it went against my flow."

1975; Mixed media; 42 × 18½ × 17 inches
Gift of the Nzingha Society, Inc., 1980
Photograph: Frank Stewart

149

Red Grooms
The Bookstore

THE HUDSON RIVER MUSEUM
YONKERS, NEW YORK

Most museums have bookstores but only the Hudson River Museum has one that is also a comic environmental artwork. In 1978, Director Richard Koshalek decided to commission an artist to redesign the museum's sales shop and in his mind, "It had to be Red Grooms."

Grooms (1937–) was known as one of New York's "happenings" artists in the late 1950s, when he staged a number of zany performances in a series of increasingly elaborate sets. By the late 1960s the sets had evolved into complex three-dimensional environments such as *The City of Chicago, The Discount Store,* and *Ruckus Rodeo.* These works were exhibited only temporarily, however; the Hudson River Museum was the first to ask Grooms for a permanently installed and functional environment.

Enclosed on four sides, Grooms's *Bookstore* has two entrances leading to a central space where books, posters, and toys are actually sold. One entrance parodies the neoclassical facade of New York's Pierpont Morgan Library; the other simulates the entrance to Mendoza's Book Company, a lower Manhattan secondhand shop. Inside, every available surface is filled with cartoon-style painted and three-dimensional decoration. In the Morgan end, Grooms replicated the library's diamond-paned display cases and filled them with imaginary correspondence—for example, from Robert Louis Stevenson and Enrico Caruso. The Mendoza section displays another literary genre: a chaotic array of painted books with titles such as *The Woman Who Loved John Wilkes Booth* and *Queen of the Headhunters.* There are life-sized, stuffed vinyl figures of browsers, the owner of Mendoza's, a Morgan Library guard, and J. P. Morgan himself.

Reviewing Grooms's work, *New York Times* critic John Russell observes, "More perhaps than any other living American artist, Red Grooms has a genuinely popular following. . . . It must be art because it is made welcome in museums, and yet its alliances are with the circus, the fairground and the toyshop." Grooms, on the other hand, claims that he created *The Bookstore* "to bring back a little old-world stuffiness to museums again—grandeur, culture and class."

1979; Mixed media; 20 × 20 × 11 feet

Books and Articles for Further Reading

Americans and the Arts: Highlights from a 1975 Survey of Public Opinion Researched for the National Committee for Cultural Resources by the National Research Center of the Arts, Inc. 1976.

ALMA-TADEMA, SIR LAWRENCE
Swanson, Vern. *Alma-Tadema*. 1977.

BELL, LARRY
Wortz, Melinda. *Larry Bell: New Work*. Exhibition catalogue for Hudson River Museum, 1981.

BELLOWS, GEORGE
Bradier, Donald. *George Bellows and the Ashcan School of Painting*. 1971.
Morgan, Charles H. *George Bellows: Painter of America*. 1965.

BIERSTADT, ALBERT
Hendricks, Gordon. *Albert Bierstadt: Painter of the American West*. 1974.
Novak, Barbara. *American Painting of the Nineteenth Century*. 1971.

BINGHAM, GEORGE CALEB
Bloch, Maurice. *George Caleb Bingham: The Evolution of an Artist*. 1967.
Christ-Janer, Albert. *George Caleb Bingham: Frontier Painter of Missouri*. 1975

BOUGUEREAU, ADOLPHE WILLIAM
The Second Empire, 1852–1870: Art in France under Napoleon III. Exhibition catalogue for Philadelphia Museum of Art, 1978.

BRUEGEL, PIETER
Stechow, W. *Pieter Bruegel the Elder*. 1969.
The World of Pieter Bruegel. Exhibition catalogue for Metropolitan Museum of Art, 1952.

CARR, EMILY
Shadbolt, Doris. *The Art of Emily Carr*. 1979.
Tippett, Maria. *Emily Carr*. 1979.

CAILLEBOTTE, GUSTAVE
Rewald, John. *The History of Impressionism*. 1961.
Varnedoe, Kirk. "In Detail: Gustave Caillebotte's 'The Streets of Paris on a Rainy Day.' " *Portfolio*, December-January 1979.

CÉZANNE, PAUL
Rewald, John. *Paul Cézanne: A Biography*. 1968.
Schapiro, Meyer. *Modern Art: 19th and 20th Centuries*. 1979.

CHURCH, FREDERIC EDWIN
Huntington, David C. *The Landscapes of Frederic Edwin Church: A Vision of an American Era*. 1966.
Novak, Barbara. *Nature and Culture*. 1980.

COLE, THOMAS
Edmund, Dwight, and Boyle, Richard. "Rediscovery: Thomas Cole's 'Voyage of Life.' " *Art in America*, May-June 1967.
Noble, Louis L. *The Course of Empire, Voyage of Life and Other Pictures of Thomas Cole*. Edited by Elliot S. Vessell. 1964.

DEGAS, EDGAR
Boggs, Jean Sutherland. *Portraits by Degas*. 1962.
Reff, Theodore. *Degas: The Artist's Mind*. 1976.

EAKINS, THOMAS
Goodrich, Lloyd. *Thomas Eakins: His Life and Work*. 1933.
Hendricks, Gordon. *Thomas Eakins*. 1971.

ESTES, RICHARD
Canaday, John, and Arthur, John. *The Urban Landscape*. 1978.
Dean, Andrea. "Richard Estes' New York." *AIA Journal*, April 1979.

FABERGÉ PETER CARL
Snowman, Kenneth. *The Art of Carl Fabergé*. 1953.

GAINSBOROUGH, THOMAS
Hayes, John. *Thomas Gainsborough*. 1980.
Waterhouse, Ellis. *Gainsborough*. 1958.

GÉRÔME, JEAN LÉON
Ackerman, Gerald, "Gérôme." *Art News Annual*, 1968.
———. *Jean Léon Gérôme (1824–1904)*. Exhibition catalogue for Dayton Art Institute, 1972.

GOGH, VINCENT VAN
Cabanne, Pierre. *Van Gogh*. 1963.
Elgar, Frank. *Van Gogh*. 1958.

GORKY, ARSHILE
Seitz, William. *Arshile Gorky*. 1962.
Waldman, Diane. *Arshile Gorky, 1904–1948*. 1981.

GOYA, FRANCISCO DE
Gassier, Pierre, and Wilson, Juliet. *The Life and Complete Work of Francisco Goya*. 1970.
Gudiol, José. *Goya*. 1971.

GRECO, EL
Brown, Jonathan, et al. *El Greco of Toledo*. 1982.
Wethey, Harold. *El Greco and His School*. 1962.

HOMER, WINSLOW
Goodrich, Lloyd. *Winslow Homer*. 1959.
Wilmerding, John. *Winslow Homer*. 1972.

HOPPER, EDWARD
Edward Hopper: The Art and the Artist. Exhibition catalogue for Whitney Museum of American Art, 1980.
O'Doherty, Brian. *American Masters: The Voice and the Myth*. 1973.

INDIANA, ROBERT
Calas, Nicolas, and Calas, Elena. *Icons and Images of the Sixties*. 1971.
Russell, John, and Gablik, Suzi. *Pop Art Redefined*. 1969.

JOHNS, JASPER
Kozloff, Max. *Jasper Johns*. 1972.
Steinberg, Leo. *Jasper Johns*. 1963.

KANDINSKY, VASILY
Grohmann, Will. *Wassily Kandinsky: Life and Work*. 1959.
Long, Rose-Carol. *Kandinsky*. 1980.

KLEE, PAUL
Grohmann, Will. *Paul Klee*. 1954.
Haftmann, Werner. *The Mind and Work of Paul Klee*. 1954.

LARGILLIÈRE, NICOLAS DE
McCoubrey, John W. "Nicolas de Largillière," *Encyclopedia of World Art*.
Schönberger, Arno, and Soehner, Halldor. *The Rococo Age*. 1960.

LEIGHTON, LORD FREDERICK
Maas, Jeremy. *Victorian Painters*. 1969.
Ormond, Richard, and Ormond, Leonee. *Lord Leighton*. 1975.

LEUTZE, EMANUEL
Groseclose, Barbara. *Emanuel Leutze, 1816–1868: Freedom Is the Only King*. 1975.

LYSIPPOS
Richter, Gisela. *A Handbook of Greek Art*. 1960.
————. *The Sculpture and Sculptors of the Greeks*. 1970.

MANSHIP, PAUL
Murtha, Edwin. *The Sculpture of Paul Manship*. 1957.

MATISSE, HENRI
Barr, Alfred. *Henri Matisse: His Art and His Public*. 1957.
Forgey, Benjamin. "The Matisse Cutouts." *ARTnews*, December 1977.

MONET, CLAUDE
Seitz, William. *Claude Monet*. 1960.
Tucker, Paul Hayes. *Monet at Argenteuil*. 1982.

NAHL, CHARLES CHRISTIAN
Williams, H. W. *Mirror to the American Past: A Survey of American Genre Painting, 1750–1900*. 1973.

PEALE, CHARLES WILLSON
Richardson, Edgar: Hindle, Brook; and Miller, Lillian B. *Charles Willson Peale and His World*. 1982.
Sellers, Charles Coleman. *Charles Willson Peale*. 1969.

PICASSO, PABLO
Barr, Alfred. *Picasso: Fifty Years of His Art*. 1946.
Boeck, Wilhelm, and Sabartes, Jaime. *Picasso*. 1955.

PISSARRO, CAMILLE
Rewald, John. *Camille Pissarro*. 1963.
Shikes, Ralph. *Pissarro: His Life and Work*. 1980.

POLLOCK, JACKSON
O'Hara, Frank. *Jackson Pollock*. 1959.
Rubin, William. *Jackson Pollock and the Modern Tradition*. 1967.

REMBRANDT VAN RIJN
Gerson, Horst. *The Paintings of Rembrandt*. 1968.
Rosenberg, Jacob. *Rembrandt*. 1964.

RENOIR, AUGUSTE
Hanson, Lawrence. *Renoir: The Man, the Painter, and His World*. 1968.
Renoir, Jean. *Renoir: My Father*. 1962.

RIVERA, DIEGO
Myers, Bernard S. *Mexican Painting in Our Time*. 1956.
Wolfe, Bertram D. *The Fabulous Life of Diego Rivera*. 1963.

RODIN, AUGUSTE
De Caso, Jacques, and Sanders, Patricia. *Rodin's Thinker*. 1973.
Elsen, Albert. *Rodin's Gates of Hell*. 1960.

ROUSSEAU, HENRI
Rich, Daniel Catton. *Henri Rousseau.* 1969.
Vallier, Dora. *Henri Rousseau.* 1964.

RUBENS, PETER PAUL
Cabanne, Pierre. *Rubens.* 1967.
Wedgwood, Cicely V. *The World of Rubens, 1577–1640.*
1981.

SAAR, BETYE
Munro, Eleanor. *Originals: American Women Artists.*
1979.

SAMARAS, LUCAS
Kultermann, Udo. *The New Sculpture: Environments and
Assemblages.* 1967.
Townsend, Benjamin. "Albright-Knox, Buffalo: Work in
Progress." *ARTnews,* January 1967.

SARGENT, JOHN SINGER
Hoopes, Donelson. *The Private World of John Singer
Sargent.* Exhibition catalogue for Corcoran Gallery of
Art, 1964.
Ormond, Richard. *John Singer Sargent: Paintings,
Drawings, Watercolors.* 1970.

SEURAT, GEORGES
Rich, Daniel Catton. *Seurat and the Evolution of 'La
Grande Jatte.'* 1969.
Russell, John. *Seurat.* 1965.

SOTATSU, TAWARAYA, AND KOETSU, HONAMI
Leach, Bernard. *Kenzan and His Tradition.* 1969.

THOMPSON, TOM
Hibbard, Robert Hamilton. *Tom Thompson.* 1962.
Reid, Dennis. *Tom Thompson: The Jack Pine.* 1975.

TOULOUSE-LAUTREC, HENRI DE
Keller, Horst. *Toulouse-Lautrec: Painter of Paris.* 1968.
Rich, Daniel Catton. *Henri de Toulouse-Lautrec 'Au
Moulin Rouge.'* 1949.

TURNER, JOSEPH MALLORD WILLIAM
Butlin, Martin, and Joll, Evelyn. *The Paintings of J. M.
W. Turner.* 1977.
Reynolds, Graham. *Turner.* 1969.

VERMEER, JAN
Goldscheider, Ludwig. *Vermeer Paintings: Complete
Edition.* 1967.
Snow, Edward A. *A Study of Vermeer.* 1979.

WHITE, THOMAS J.
Freed, Frank. *Artists in Wood.* 1970.

Works by Unknown Artists

ARCHANGEL RAPHAEL
Pope-Hennessy, John. *An Introduction to Italian
Sculpture.* 1972.

KANSAS CRIB QUILT
Johnson, Bruce. *A Child's Comfort.* 1977.

LIBATION DISH OF DARIUS THE GREAT
Frankfort, Henri. *The Art and Architecture of the Ancient
Orient.* 1955.

PRAYER RUG WITH THREE ARCHES
Schurmann, Ulrich. *Oriental Carpets.* 1979.
Yetkin, Serare. *Early Caucasian Carpets in Turkey.* 1978.

QUILLED BUCKSKIN SHIRT
Coe, Ralph T. *Sacred Circles.* Exhibition catalogue for
Hayward Gallery, 1977.
Schneider, Richard. *Crafts of the North American Indians.*
1972.

TIBETAN TEMPLE HANGING
Lumir, Jisl. *Tibetan Art.* 1961.
Reynolds, Valrae. *Tibet: A Lost World.* Exhibition
catalogue for American Federation of the Arts and
Newark Museum, 1978.

THE UNICORN IN CAPTIVITY
Freeman, Margaret B. *The Unicorn Tapestries.* 1976.
Verlet, Pierre. *The Book of Tapestry.* 1978.

Index of Museums and Galleries

Index of Artists

Artnews Books

Chairman: Milton Esterow
President and Editor-in-Chief: John L. Hochmann
Managing Editor: Ray F. Patient

Composition: Dix Type Co., Syracuse, New York
Printing and binding: Mandarin Offset International, Ltd., Hong Kong

Designer: Katy Homans
Art Assistant: John Di Re